Living Off the Land

By Richard P. Emanuel

ALASKA GEOGRAPHIC® Volume 27, Number 4, 2000

EDITOR
Penny Rennick

PRODUCTION DIRECTOR
Kathy Doogan

ASSOCIATE EDITOR
Susan Beeman

MARKETING DIRECTOR
Mark Weber

ADMINISTRATIVE ASSISTANT
Melanie Britton

ISBN: 1-56661-050-8

PRICE TO NON-MEMBERS THIS ISSUE: $21.95

PRINTED IN U.S.A.

POSTMASTER:
Send address changes to:

ALASKA GEOGRAPHIC®
P.O. Box 93370
Anchorage, Alaska 99509-3370

COVER: *Richard Hayden Sr., longtime resident of the state, checks his subsistence net on the Sheenjek River in northeast Alaska.* (Mark Kelley)

PREVIOUS PAGE: *Healthy caribou are an important source of lean meat for many rural Alaskans.* (Patrick Endres)

FACING PAGE: *Amos Green holds strips of beluga whale blubber at a subsistence camp on the shore of Kotzebue Sound near the Tukrok River.* (Fred Hirschmann)

ALASKA GEOGRAPHIC® (ISSN 0361-1353) is published quarterly by The Alaska Geographic Society, 639 West International Airport Rd. #38, Anchorage, AK 99518. Periodicals postage paid at Anchorage, Alaska, and additional mailing offices. Copyright © 2000 The Alaska Geographic Society. All rights reserved. Registered trademark: Alaska Geographic, ISSN 0361-1353; key title Alaska Geographic. This issue published Dec. 2000.

THE ALASKA GEOGRAPHIC SOCIETY is a non-profit, educational organization dedicated to improving geographic understanding of Alaska and the North, putting geography back in the classroom and exploring new methods of teaching and learning.

MEMBERS RECEIVE *ALASKA GEOGRAPHIC®*, a high-quality, colorful quarterly that devotes each issue to monographic, in-depth coverage of a specific northern region or resource-oriented subject. Back issues are also available (see p. 96). Membership is $49 ($59 to non-U.S. addresses) per year. To order or to request a free catalog of back issues, contact: Alaska Geographic Society, P.O. Box 93370, Anchorage, AK 99509-3370; phone (907) 562-0164 or toll free (888) 255-6697, fax (907) 562-0479, e-mail: akgeo@akgeo.com. A complete listing of our back issues, maps and other products can also be found on our website at www.akgeo.com.

SUBMITTING PHOTOGRAPHS: Those interested in submitting photos for possible publication should write for a list of upcoming topics or other photo needs and a copy of our editorial guidelines. We cannot be responsible for unsolicited submissions. Please note that any submission not accompanied by sufficient postage for return by certified mail will be returned by regular mail.

CHANGE OF ADDRESS: When you move, the post office may not automatically forward your *ALASKA GEOGRAPHIC®*. To ensure continuous service, please notify us at least six weeks before moving. Send your new address and membership number or a mailing label from a recent issue of *ALASKA GEOGRAPHIC®* to: Address Change, Alaska Geographic Society, Box 93370, Anchorage, AK 99509-3370.

If your issue is returned to us by the post office because it is undeliverable, we will contact you to ask if you wish to receive a replacement for a small fee to cover the cost of additional postage to reship the issue.

COLOR SEPARATIONS: Graphic Chromatics
PRINTING: Banta Publications Group / Hart Press

The Library of Congress has cataloged this serial publication as follows:

Alaska Geographic. v.1-
  [Anchorage, Alaska Geographic Society] 1972-
  v. ill. (part col.). 23 x 31 cm.
  Quarterly
  Official publication of The Alaska Geographic Society.
  Key title: Alaska geographic, ISSN 0361-1353.

  1. Alaska—Description and travel—1959-
  —Periodicals. I. Alaska Geographic Society.

F901.A266   917.98'04'505   72-92087

Library of Congress 75[79112] MARC-S.

ABOUT THIS ISSUE:

More than 100,000 people live in Alaska's remote areas, far from the grocery stores of bigger towns and cities. They take advantage of food the land provides, whether mammal, fish, bird, or plant. Each region of the state has its specific resources: whales and seals in the northern and western sections; moose and berries in the interior; salmon in the southwest; and on around the state.

Dick Emanuel, author of other *ALASKA GEOGRAPHIC®* books, including *Steve McCutcheon's Alaska* and *The Golden Gamble*, gives readers an overview of the subsistence lifestyle and includes interviews with people who make the Bush their home. Sidebars written by residents of Petersburg, Kotzebue, Nikolski, Uganik Bay on Kodiak Island, and other small communities offer firsthand accounts of hunting, picking berries, harvesting greens, and the many other activities of getting food from the land.

We'd like to thank Dr. Don Kramer of the University of Alaska Marine Advisory Program for detailed help with the common and scientific names of fish and marine invertebrates; Anore Jones, who graciously let us excerpt from her book *Nauriat Niginaqtuat, Plants That We Eat* (1983); and the Alaska Native Language Center for guidance in the spelling of Native words.

EDITOR'S NOTE: In this text we have tried to use the most common spelling for Alaska Native words, but readers should note that Alaska Native languages are still evolving. Preferred spellings change, and sometimes even preferred words. In this issue, *Yupik* refers to the three Yupik languages or to a Siberian Yupik person. *Yup'ik* refers to Central Yup'ik, the people living on the Yukon-Kuskokwim Delta. The plural of *Yupik* and *Yup'ik* is *Yupiit*. Farther north, many Inupiat (singular Inupiaq) people are adopting the term *Inuit* to refer to themselves. *Inupiaq* is also the language the Inupiat speak.

CONTENTS

Living Off the Land

By Richard P. Emanuel

Seasons of Earth and Sea

To live off the land and water in Alaska is to follow the ceaseless flow of the seasons, to live a life whose rhythms are palpable in the very earth, sea, and sky.

George Noongwook lives in Savoonga, on St. Lawrence Island, in the Bering Sea. For twenty-first-century Siberian Yupiks like Noongwook, as for generations before them, the pulse of the year is laid down in cycles of daylight and darkness, in the advance and retreat of sea ice, in swirling waves of seabirds, walrus, whales, seals, seaweed, and berries brought forth upon and around their island.

The result is a kind of calendar according to which the St. Lawrence Islander's year unfolds.

"January is mostly sealing — ringed seals, spotted seals, bearded seals. That goes through January, February, March," Noongwook begins. "April and part of May concentrate on bowhead whaling. May and June are spent hunting mostly walrus.

"Seabird hunting is done in April and May, in conjunction with whaling or walrus hunting," Noongwook continues. "Waterfowl are in late spring or in late fall.

"Reindeer are rounded up and corralled every summer, usually in the first week of July. The reindeer are in their velvet antler stage and there are Asian markets that will buy those antlers. We'll take a few reindeer to eat, too.

"July through early October is mostly fishing — halibut fishing, salmon fishing, trout fishing, whitefish. That runs until the lakes and rivers are pretty much frozen.

"Picking greens is done in July and August, too, a whole range of roots and mushrooms, wild potatoes, wild celery, sourdock for salads. I don't know the English names for a lot of the plants that we gather. Berries are done in August and September, too. In the fall, there is stuff from the seafloor we also gather: seaweeds and kelp that are washed up on the beach, sea plants and animals that cling to the rocks, sea squirts.

"Then when the north wind blows in October, November, December, sealing begins again. Of course, whenever we run across a polar bear, we'll take one of those, especially if it's a good one, around five or six feet."

FACING PAGE: *Siberian Yupik whalers from Gambell on the northwest tip of St. Lawrence Island use a combination of sail and paddle to move their skinboat through the Bering Sea. (Chlaus Lotscher)*

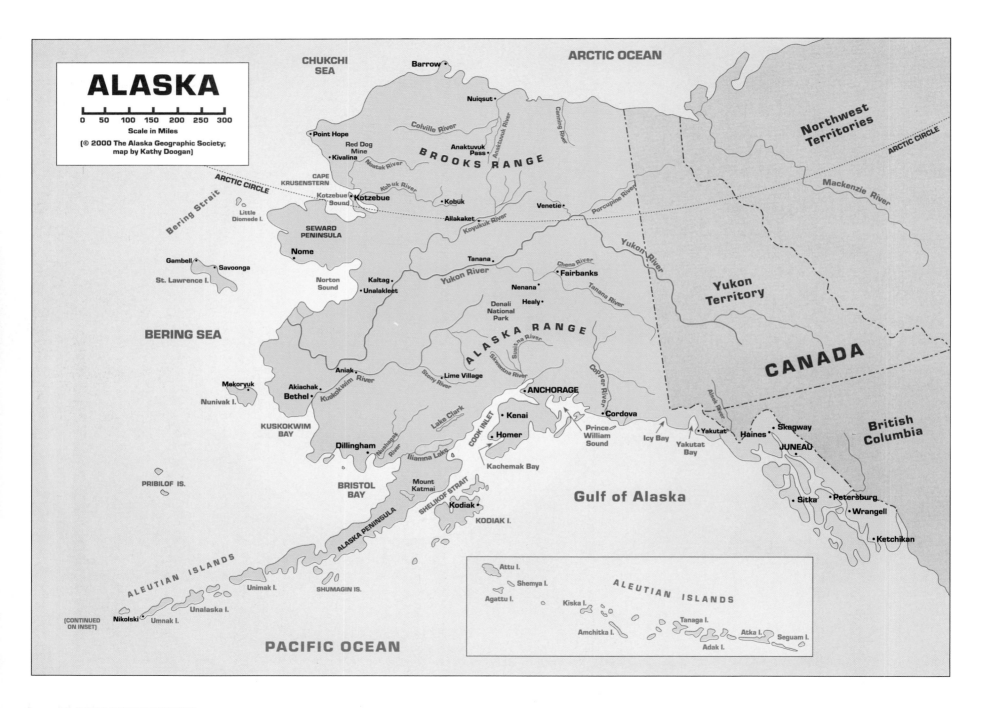

ALASKA

Scale in Miles
0 50 100 150 200 250 300

(© 2000 The Alaska Geographic Society;
map by Kathy Doogan)

CHUKCHI SEA

ARCTIC OCEAN

Barrow

Nuiqsut

Colville River

Canning River

Point Hope

Red Dog Mine

Kivalina

Anaktuvuk Pass

Anaktuvuk River

BROOKS RANGE

Noatak River

Northwest Territories

ARCTIC CIRCLE

Mackenzie River

CAPE KRUSENSTERN

Kobuk River

ARCTIC CIRCLE

Kotzebue Sound

Kotzebue

Kobuk

Allakaket

Venetie

Porcupine River

Koyukuk River

Bering Strait

Little Diomede I.

SEWARD PENINSULA

Yukon River

Gambell

Savoonga

St. Lawrence I.

Nome

Norton Sound

Kaltag

Unalakleet

Tanana

Chena River

Fairbanks

Nenana

Healy

Yukon River

Tanana River

Yukon Territory

BERING SEA

Denali National Park

ALASKA RANGE

Susitna River

CANADA

Mekoryuk

Aniak

Lime Village

Stony River

Skwentna River

Copper River

Alsek River

Akiachak

Bethel

Kuskokwim River

Nunivak I.

Lake Clark

ANCHORAGE

Cordova

Kenai

Prince William Sound

Icy Bay

Yakutat

Haines

Skagway

British Columbia

KUSKOKWIM BAY

Dillingham

Nushagak River

Iliamna Lake

COOK INLET

Homer

Kachemak Bay

Yakutat Bay

JUNEAU

PRIBILOF IS.

BRISTOL BAY

Mount Katmai

SHELIKOF STRAIT

Kodiak

Gulf of Alaska

Sitka

Petersburg

Wrangell

KODIAK I.

Ketchikan

ALEUTIAN ISLANDS

Unimak I.

SHUMAGIN IS.

Attu I.

Shemya I.

ALEUTIAN ISLANDS

(CONTINUED ON INSET)

Nikolski

Umnak I.

Unalaska I.

Agattu I.

Kiska I.

Tanaga I.

Amchitka I.

Atka I.

Seguam I.

Adak I.

PACIFIC OCEAN

Seth and Kole Kantner follow their dad to a trap site in the Kobuk River valley. (Courtesy of Seth Kantner)

Throughout rural Alaska, details of the local calendar differ, but bush Alaskans everywhere live close to the land. They watch and await opportunity, adapt and accept what comes. When migrating birds arrive early or when the ice comes late, when the polar bear presents itself, the hunter takes what is borne on the currents of time.

The pace of life in urban Alaska is very different. There is a joke told about Alaska's largest city: The great thing about Anchorage, the gibe goes, is that it is so close to Alaska.

The humor is sardonic if you live in the Bush, a bit rueful if you're an urban Alaskan. Either way, it reveals a prevalent view of modern Alaska as a society divided: There is urban Alaska, where people drive to jobs in banks and retail stores, dine in restaurants and frequent theaters, shopping malls, and espresso bars. Then there is the "real" Alaska, where self-reliant men and women live off the land, feasting on salmon, moose, and berries in handcrafted homes warmed by cords of split and seasoned firewood.

As with most humor, buried in the punch line of the old joke is a kernel of truth. Life in urban Alaska at the dawn of the twenty-first century is much like life in other American cities, while rural Alaska is unlikely to be confused with anyplace else in the United States. True, satellite dishes and Internet hook-ups

ABOVE, LEFT: *Alaska's natural resources fill some medicinal as well as food requirements. Here Nancy Wilson gathers plants near Dillingham to augment her medicine cabinet. (Roy Corral)*

ABOVE: *Elder Bill Ermeloff, 81, cuts up a halibut he caught in Nikolski Bay. Meat from the bottom of the halibut is used for soups and chowders, the top side is for steaks. Kaarina Stamm, wife of Nikolski's postmaster, fries the steaks in butter or bakes them in the oven with a couple tablespoons of lemon juice. (Kaarina Stamm)*

are increasingly common in the Bush. But alongside them are skinboats, racks for drying fish, and the tanned pelts of grizzly bears.

Modern Alaska is truly a pluralistic society, home to a number of distinct cultures and ways of life existing side by side. Experts classify even the economic systems of urban and rural Alaska differently. Urban Alaskans do battle each day in a capitalist market economy that

is increasingly global. In bush Alaska, a mixed subsistence-cash economy predominates, in which limited cash income supports and augments hunting, fishing, and other ways of living directly off the land.

There are deep differences between urban and rural Alaska, yet the two worlds are interpenetrating and some people move comfortably between them. In some ways the differences between

Sea Lovage

Sea lovage (*Ligusticum scoticum*) leaves and stems are best when picked in early spring. They can be eaten raw dipped in seal oil. Other ways to fix them are raw in salads and boiled as a hot green to eat with butter. Aleuts and Southeast residents boil them with meat, especially fish. The spicy flavor goes out of the leaves and into the fish as they cook, making both taste better. The leaves and fish are drained and eaten together, hot or cold, with seal oil. Some people find the leaves too sweet when fixed this way.

— Adapted from Nauriat Niginaqtuat (1983)

BELOW: *Fish racks loaded with drying salmon brighten the shore of Iliamna Lake. Fish, chiefly salmon, are one of the mainstays of Alaska's rural lifestyle. Where salmon are not readily available, residents look to other species of fish to fill their pantry. Only in the far north where caribou are much more common do salmon play a secondary role in feeding the people. (Roz Goodman)*

BELOW, RIGHT: *Residents of Arctic Village in Northeast Alaska scan the Chandalar River valley during an autumn moose hunt. The Chandalar flows south out of the Brooks Range to join the Yukon River 20 miles northwest of the community of Fort Yukon. (Roy Corral)*

city and Bush are more apparent than real. In Alaska, even the urban market economy is firmly rooted in the land and sea: in oil and mining, commercial fishing, timber, tourism, and the management of government lands. Many urban Alaskans are avid anglers and hunters. Many kayak, climb, ski, camp, hike, or build backcountry cabins. One way or another, Alaskans are bound body and soul to the magnificent land they share.

For most Alaskans, and for a great many others, there is a romance in the notion of living off the land. Deep in the hearts of many urban Alaskans there lurks a spark of desire to chuck the modern marketplace and move into the Bush to do what hardy souls did generations ago, what Alaska Natives have done for thousands of years, what more than 100,000 Alaskans do today: to wrest a living from wild resources through one's own efforts, to live off northern waters and land.

Wild Resources

One in five Alaskans today lives in rural areas, about 125,000 people in more than 250 communities. Most rural settlements are off the road network and comprise fewer than 500 people. A majority are predominantly Native villages. In a state whose population is 15 percent Native, nearly half of all rural Alaskans are Alaska Natives.

Nowhere in the United States is there such a strong reliance on wild food and resources as in rural Alaska. Virtually everyone in the region joins in the area's mixed subsistence-cash economy, if not directly through hunting and fishing at least through widespread sharing of food. The Subsistence Division of the Alaska Department of Fish and Game (ADFG) has tracked the harvest of wild resources for more than 20 years. Rural Alaskans harvest roughly 45 million pounds of wild food annually, an average of about 375 pounds per person. Wild foods supply about a third of the caloric requirements of rural Alaskans and an overabundance of protein, well over twice the mean daily protein requirement. By comparison, the average American purchases 222 pounds of store-bought meat, poultry, and fish each year, about 16 percent of a total of 1,370 pounds of food.

There are wide regional variations in the amount of wild foods consumed in the state. The harvest of wild food in Western and rural Interior Alaska is more than 600 pounds per person annually. The figure exceeds 500 pounds in the Arctic. Residents of the Aleutians and Southwest Alaska consume an average of 370 pounds of wild food per year. On Kodiak Island and in rural Southcentral and Southeast Alaska, per capita consumption ranges between 150 and 180 pounds annually.

Wild foods taken by rural Alaskans include fish, land and marine mammals, shellfish, birds, eggs, and plants. Statewide, fish are by far the greatest part of the harvest, about 60 percent of the total by weight. Salmon, halibut, herring, and whitefish comprise the bulk of the catch. Land mammals —

Moose stew bubbles over an open fire during a potlatch at the Athabaskan community of Allakaket, population 204. Alatna, an Inupiat Eskimo community of 34, and Allakaket face each other on opposite banks of the Yukon River near its junction with the Alatna River. (Roy Corral)

Stella Zeeder shows off green sea urchins she collected near Akhiok, an Alutiiq community, population 101, near the southern tip of Kodiak Island. (Roy Corral)

chiefly moose and caribou but including bear, deer, mountain goat, Dall sheep, and beaver — make up 20 percent of the take by weight. Bowhead and beluga whales, sea lions, seals, and walrus comprise the marine mammal catch, some 14 percent of the statewide total. By treaty and law, only Natives may take marine mammals, although non-commercial sharing is traditional and accepted. Birds, shellfish and other invertebrates, and plants, notably berries, fill out the remaining 6 percent of the rural harvest of wild food.

Just as the amount of wild food consumed varies from place to place, so do the kinds of food differ. Inupiat and Yupik Natives of the Arctic and Bering Sea coasts harvest the most marine mammals (just over 100 pounds per person per year), while Interior Athabaskans, far from the sea, take none. Southeast and Aleutian residents take the fewest land mammals while Arctic, Western, and Interior residents, with ready access to moose and caribou, take the most (more than 100 pounds per capita).

Other differences are more local, based on both availability and tradition. In coastal areas, shellfish and invertebrates such as clams exposed by low tide offer

Eating Alaska's wild foods can sometimes be dangerous. Every year, several people in remote areas are treated for botulism, a potentially deadly illness contracted from eating spoiled or improperly preserved food.

Botulism was originally called "sausage poisoning" when six people in Wildbad, Germany died in 1793 after eating blood sausage. A local health officer, Justinius Kerner, studied hundreds of subsequent cases, dubbing the sickness "botulism," after the Latin word for sausage, "botulus." Scientists later discovered that botulism is caused by spore-producing bacteria that can contaminate food.

Traditional methods of preserving and storing some Alaska Native foods can let *Clostridium botulinum* run rampant, making villagers sick with gastrointestinal, urinary, neurological, and muscular difficulties, sometimes resulting in death. Food spoilage, whether intentional or not, also opens the door to botulism.

Fermented salmon heads (stink heads) are a delicacy among some Yupik people of Western Alaska. Before the advent of sealable plastic bags and barrels, Natives made stink heads by burying salmon heads in moss-lined pits in the ground. Left all summer, the fish was dug up when ready, kneaded into a pasty texture, and eaten.

Today, stink heads and stink eggs (salmon eggs) are still fermented, but the anaerobic conditions of modern, closed containers such as plastic buckets and plastic bags increase the likelihood of the botulin toxin forming.

Some food storage conditions can also lead to illness or death from botulism. Root cellars don't always keep meat completely frozen, allowing bacteria to grow. Those living without electricity for freezers must rely on this traditional cold storage method to preserve meat throughout the year. Even dried meat and fish can become rancid if not stored properly.

Most cases of botulism in Alaska come from eating seal oil or salmon eggs, and the number of outbreaks is highest in July, the season when these two items are most abundant statewide.

Botulism will grow in low-acid foods such as meat, fish, and vegetables; where no air is present; where the temperature is higher than 38 degrees Fahrenheit; and in foods stored too long. To avoid getting botulism, store and process food properly. Refrigerate, freeze, can or jar with a pressure cooker, or dry meat and fish. For fermenting, use cloth or paper that breathes for wrapping, not plastic. Always boil suspected foods 15 minutes, and as the saying goes, when in doubt — throw it out!

ABOVE: *A red fox pelt is stretched on a board after skinning. To remove the pelt, the trapper first makes a slit down the back of each hind leg to the anus and from the front paws to the elbows, then hangs the animal by a hind foot, peeling the pelt down toward the head. Using small strokes with a knife, the trapper cuts the pelt from the body, being careful not to nick the pelt. (Alissa Crandall)*

FACING PAGE: *Glaucous-winged gull eggs are exposed to predators and egg-collecting on this rocky perch overlooking Sitkalidak Strait off Kodiak's southeastern shore. In parts of Alaska bird eggs provide refreshing variety in the rural diet. (Chlaus Lotscher)*

nutritious treats. On St. Lawrence Island, the region's profusion of birds attracts hunters. A 1996 survey showed that the island's 1,300 residents took some 20,000 birds of 26 species, plus more than 14,000 eggs.

As impressive as the subsistence harvest is, it is a modest part of the total take of Alaska wildlife. Commercial fishing statewide dwarfs sport and subsistence hunting and fishing combined. A 1998 report by ADFG estimates that commercial fisheries take roughly 2 billion pounds per year from Alaska waters, or nearly 97 percent of the

total weight of fish and wildlife harvested in Alaska. Sport fishing and hunting account for 18 million pounds annually, or 1 percent of the total harvest. Rural subsistence takes another 45 million pounds, or some 2.2 percent.

If commercial fishing is the hungry giant in the competition for wild resources, its impact depends on the resource and where it is found. There is no commercial fishery in the Arctic Ocean, for instance, and no commercial taking of marine mammals anywhere in Alaska. Competition for salmon is another matter. Commercial fishing in Alaska powerfully affects freshwater fish stocks by intercepting salmon and other anadromous species at sea, before they can return to spawn in streams across the state.

In contrast to fishing, commercial activities have little direct impact on hunting. There is no commercial hunting, except for guided hunts, which require sport licenses of hunters. Chartered fishing boats similarly require sport licenses of anglers.

Rural Alaskans sustain themselves with more than fish and game, however. There are berries to pick when ripe, wild roots and edible herbs to gather. Many bush homes include a large garden. And then there is wood.

Wood is used to smoke meat or fish, both to flavor and preserve the flesh. Cabins and other buildings, fish racks, lean-tos, and boats are built with wood. Firewood heats many homes, especially in isolated locations, although in most villages, fuel oil has replaced firewood for primary heating.

Trappers harvest fur-bearing animals and turn their furs into frost-resistant ruffs on parkas and into warm linings in *mukluks* (boots). Other furs are sold for cash. Skins of caribou and seals may be sewn into clothing; skins of walrus and seals may be stretched over wooden boat frames.

Still other wild resources provide materials for traditional arts and crafts: ivory, soapstone, and jade for carving, bark for masks, grass for weaving into

A fisherman casts a net for herring during a sac roe subsistence opening in Sitka Sound in Southeast Alaska. (Harry M. Walker)

Mekoryuk residents James Whitman (left), Linda Jean Richards (center) and Joel John butcher a muskox on Nunivak Island. The last muskoxen indigenous to Alaska were killed in the mid-1800s. To restore the species, muskoxen were reintroduced to Alaska in the 1930s. Thirty-one animals were transported from Fairbanks to Nunivak in 1935. After a time, the island herd prospered and individuals were taken from that herd for reintroduction to other parts of their historical range in western and northern Alaska. (Daryl Kyra Lee)

fine mats and baskets. Plants and minerals yield pigments and dyes. For those with knowledge, patience, and skill, nature's storehouse is stocked with goods of infinite variety, beauty, and use.

Drying and Smoking Salmon Heads

EDITOR'S NOTE: *This excerpt is from* How To Split, Dry And Smoke Salmon *(1982) by Anecia Breiby, a project of the Adult Literacy Laboratory at Anchorage Community College. Anecia learned how to process salmon from her mother, Anita Iyuptulla Lopez, who was born at Black Point on the Nushagak River in Southwest Alaska.*

To prepare salmon heads for drying and smoking, open the gill cover of the fish. Exposed gills should be facing you. Cut through the connecting tissue at the front of the head and remove the gills from the head. Cut through the nape to sever the tips from the head. Cut between the lower lip at the front, then cut down on either side of the nose to remove the cartilage. However, make sure not to cut through the skin at the back of the head. The object is to have the head lie flat.

The section you removed from the head is the cartilage of the nose and is delicious cooked in a soup. It has a nutty consistency.

Once the cartilage is removed, turn the head over and cut two slits in the cheeks. With the point of the knife, cut through the skin so you will have a hole in which to attach a string. Cut a second head in the same manner so you can hang two from the same string.

— *Anecia Breiby*

Salmon heads destined for fermentation lie piled together, soon to become a sour mush that some Yupik consider a delicacy. (Greg Syverson)

Lessons From A Vanished Land

By Robert Belous

EDITOR'S NOTE: *Writer-photographer Bob Belous has traveled extensively in Northwest Alaska and has reported on numerous Alaska subjects since 1968. He spent 11 years in the Anchorage office of the National Park Service. Spelling of Alaska Native words is evolving; for the most part we have followed spellings provided by the author, but readers should note that authorities at the Alaska Native Language Center in Fairbanks assign "q" to some words formerly spelled with "k," i.e.* uqsruq *for seal oil. The word* Tagiumsinaaqmiit *is now spelled* Tagium Sinaaqmiut, allpa *is now* alpa, uksruk *is* uqsruq.*

Deep in the marrow of remote villages are food-gathering skills derived from a time when Alaska was still parting from Asia. Sharpened by centuries of experiment and invention, and seasoned with periodic tragedy, these ancient strategies can appear quaint, sometimes deceptive, but are often deadly serious. These are skills uniquely crafted to sustain life at the outermost edges of human habitat.

Some of the most arcane techniques for living off the land evolved in regions of Alaska where the land has now disappeared. Early hunters of 14,000 years ago followed big game quarry across a land bridge destined for submergence. What began as a 900-mile-wide plain (at 580,000 square miles, it was twice the size of Texas) once supported large mammals, such as bison, wapiti, camel, red deer, and woolly mammoth. But the plain would one day become a sea floor with walrus and whales swimming above. And these early

FAR LEFT: A crested auklet is trapped in a hunter's net. Cliff-dwelling birds provide some of the first fresh meat of the year for residents of the Bering and Chukchi sea coasts. (Robert Belous)

LEFT: Savoonga elder Alexander Akeya snatches auklets from the air in an ages-old method of capture on St. Lawrence Island. (Robert Belous)

hunters, called Paleo-Indians, would pass deeper into North America, leaving little evidence of dependency upon fishing or bird life or any diversity in their survival skills.

The ensuing millennia brought epochal change in human history. As massive land glaciers melted, the rising Pacific Ocean advanced northward into what is now the Bering and Chukchi seas. Long-hidden lagoons, estuaries, sounds, and bays were unlocked from the ice. Fresh habitats lured sea mammals, fish, waterfowl and pelagic birds. Early Asiatic people then living along the land bridge's Pacific Rim soon followed the bounty along the lengthening shoreline. These sea-savvy migrants introduced a palette of new and lasting techniques for survival.

This precursor of today's Eskimo culture brought forth new languages, lifeways, and perfected skills for offshore harvest of sea mammals and bird life, along with myriad fishing techniques and exploitation of the intertidal zone. Though both Bering Sea coasts were inhabited by early Eskimos, the slightly milder climate and increased productivity of the Alaska perimeter favored larger populations. This northward wave of highly adaptive hunter-gatherers began what is now called the Northern Maritime

A seal hunter jumps overflow in the Chukchi Sea. Even with modern implements, ice pack seal hunting requires thorough understanding of animal behavior, sea ice, wind, and weather, for which there is no textbook. Cultural continuity of the Tagiumsinaaqmiit, *the seafront-living Eskimos, is the sole purveyor of this complex skill. (Robert Belous)*

Tradition. Successive stages would ultimately extend the Eskimo culture and its evolving languages across the top of North America, as far east as Greenland.

A mere 272 years ago, when Danish explorer Vitus Bering sailed through the strait that now bears his name, the Eskimo people had successfully gleaned a living from this harsh environment for upwards of 4,000 years. Many of their time-tested methods and menus work today.

To hunt the seas of the Bering and Chukchi today, residents of Northwest Alaska must know how to read the sea and to listen to the life around them. Scanning the ice pack from shoreline vantage points is one of the rites of spring among hunters in coastal villages. The arrival of seal, walrus, or whale provides an opportunity for the first fresh meat of the year. But the eyes of a Point Hope or Wainwright hunter

strain not just to see the animals but also for signs of *puguroak*, the steam-fog of open water. *Puguroak* forms along cracks and leads in the shifting ice pack. Such tendrils of steam mark a possible route for skinboats to reach the quarry, and return. But only the experienced eye will select a lead that will give access and not become an icy trap, turning a skinboat into matchsticks and stranding the hunters.

Similarly, each spring St. Lawrence Island's walrus hunters watch keenly for dark patches on

low-scudding clouds. These shadows mark pockets of open water that form as the north-flowing ice pack parts around the island, only to regather on its leeward side. During this time, hunters maintain full-alert status because thousands of walrus will drift by the island on their northbound migration, and 50 percent of the year's harvest for the villages of Savoonga and Gambell will likely take place in 10 days. Subtracting time for impassable ice pack and bad weather, the harvest may be less

Distant mountains guide hunters towing this ugruk *or bearded seal back to shore. The largest of Alaska's true seals, bearded seals weigh an average of 475 pounds in summer and 750 pounds in winter. (Robert Belous)*

than one week. This natural clock is well-known to a culture that resides on an island that was once a modest upland near the middle of the Bering Land Bridge.

Farther north, an *umiak* full of Little Diomede Island walrus hunters, fog-bound in Bering Strait, can set a homeward course without a compass. They listen for trumpeting calls from long skeins of sandhill cranes, flying in bright sunlight just above the fog banks. The cranes' flight is invariably east-to-west across the strait, as the birds head to spring nesting grounds in Siberia. Thus their trumpeting calls become a compass bearing. Closer to Little Diomede, the piercing cries and telltale aroma from colonies of cliff-nesting kittiwakes and murres guide the hunters to their tiny village.

Dance and drum-chanting traditionally carry instructive legends to young hunters of Savoonga and Gambell. The stories are told in *Suk*, an Eskimo dialect of Siberian Yupik. Amid almost hypnotic drum-chanting, elders tell of hunting exploits and the skills — and good luck — needed for success and survival. But failure and tragedy are also depicted, for St. Lawrence Island has known hardship and widespread starvation, even in historic times.

During a visit to the island in 1880, Capt. C. L. Hooper of the U.S. Revenue Cutter *Corwin* reported that famine and disease during the winter of 1878-1879 led to the death of 1,000 people from an estimated island population of 1,500. Likely causes range from alcohol introduced by whaling crews to impassable barriers of pack ice that prevented the autumn walrus harvest. Even earthquakes have been suggested. But there is also a telling note in the journal of Ivan Petroff (1898) that cites four commercial steamers and 36 sailing craft collecting 15,000 pounds of tusk ivory during the same period. This would account for about 10,000 walrus being eliminated from Bering Sea stocks. Also, Eskimo assistance was often paid for with alcohol. Whatever the causes, the island's population has yet to recover from this loss of 120 years ago.

Prehistory also offers its grim lesson. An archaeological excavation in 1974 at St. Lawrence Island's Cape Kialegak crossed several time-strata of human occupation. Now uninhabited, the cape had long been a large village site, with layer upon layer of middens. One large cache of frozen walrus and whale meat, radiocarbon dated to 1,000 A.D., suggested a time of relative plenty. But a deeper layer, where sea ice had scoured a cliff face, revealed a still-frozen human body that told a different story.

With full cooperation of village elders, the frozen and intact remains of a 50-year-old woman were analyzed by radiocarbon dating and found to be 1,610 years old. On-site evidence suggests that she died by asphyxiation while buried beneath the mass of a collapsed sod house. Tools and household items typical of the Old Bering Sea period of Eskimo prehistory were found in association with her entombment. Yet the only contents found in her well-preserved stomach were bits of moss (*Meesia triquetra*), common to the island's wet tundra, but not known as food. Nothing of nourishing value was detected in her immediate surroundings.

Thus the body of a woman weakened by starvation leads to a cautious conclusion. No sign of help for her entrapment further suggests either a vacant village, or people too weak to assist. There is even some chance that eating the common moss might have

had a mild sedative effect, easing fatigue, cold, and dire hunger.

"The Frozen Lady" yielded much first-of-its-kind evidence of living off the land. Her lungs showed signs of carbon inhalation, telling of a lifetime spent cooking over open fires and seal oil lamps. Today's diagnosis would be emphysema. While bone mass appeared normal, she had notable scoliosis (curvature of the spine). Inspection by ultra-violet light revealed tattooing on both forearms and hands with a pattern of dots and stripes, punctuated with a butterflylike, or flanged heart, symbol. She was without facial tattooing.

But it was her cardiovascular system that placed her in league with today's high-stress, high-cholesterol society. The well-preserved body showed clear signs of coronary artery disease, or atherosclerosis. This malady has been documented as far back as dynastic Egypt. But the Frozen Lady verified its presence in prehistoric Eskimo culture. Her body chemistry also showed detectable levels of mercury. While this would not be surprising for people currently on

a diet rich in sea mammals, to find levels of methyl mercury reaching one-half of current levels in an individual dwelling in remote arctic environs early in the Christian Era has helped establish a new benchmark for the evolution of human health.

In 1977, the Frozen Lady's remains were quietly reinterred by village elders from Savoonga, at a site known only to them.

Reminders of famine tend to sharpen inventive skills for survival. At a glance, swift-flying seabirds would appear ludicrously safe from a hunter armed only

with a handheld net, mounted on a clumsy, eight-foot pole. But a seasoned Eskimo's keen observation — and ability to think like a crested auklet — has silently plucked these swift birds out of the sky for countless generations.

Auklets return to their rock-crevice nests by flying into the wind, then abruptly upward at the rim of a seacliff. The adroit hunter places himself slightly upwind of the nest, then waits for that instant in which the returning bird is slowed by wind-spill over the rock crest. Rising from a crouch, the hunter draws

As artful as it is ingenious, the harpoon head emerged about 4,000 years ago amid the sea-faring Eskimos of Beringia. (Robert Belous)

the hovering bird's attention, while at the same time lifting the net on the bird's opposite side. The effect is like a pair of pincers. As the auklet turns away from the hunter, it entangles itself in the advancing net. About one in five attempts will catch an auklet. And it can be the first fresh meat of spring if sea mammal hunts are poor.

In the *Inupiaq* language, the term *Tagiumsinaaqmiit* refers to Eskimos who've made their living along the seafront. They are expert at gleaning traditional foods from the open ice pack of the Chukchi Sea, and from along its lagoons and beach bluffs. These hunters venture miles offshore into shifting ice floes from Sealing Point, at Cape Krusenstern, a northern knee in the coastline of Kotzebue Sound. Cape Krusenstern is an unrivaled archaeological site with 114 beach ridges holding an unbroken chronology of Eskimo occupation for the past 5,000 years. Just inland from today's beachline, for example, excavations revealed ancient housepits, tools, and artifacts, including the eight-inch stone lance blades that are the distinctive sign of the Old Whaling culture, which launched from the seafront of its day in 1,800 B.C.

Shooting a 600-pound *ugruk* dead with a single shot from a modern rifle, the task of today's hunter, is a modest chore compared to stalking prey by

FAR LEFT: *Carrie Uhl prepares* qiaq, *the outer covering of seal intestines, at Sealing Point along Kotzebue Sound. Inupiat of Northwest Alaska relish this delicacy, which is chopped and eaten raw. Another staple in rural Alaskans' diets is seal oil. Oil rendered from* ugruk *is known as* uqsruq. *(Robert Belous)*

LEFT: *Napaaqtuq, an elder who recalled the days of hunting prior to the widespread use of rifles at Sealing Point, instructs younger family members in the preparation of* qiaq. *(Robert Belous)*

crawling toward it with a primitive harpoon, the challenge facing a prehistoric hunter. But even today getting home safely with the *ugruk* still calls for understanding seal physiology, terrain, weather, even signals of geography.

A dead *ugruk* will sink like a stone. So hunters make a small hole at the lower throat and blow air, not into the lungs but into the layer between hide and meat, until the carcass is buoyant. They plug and wrap the hole, using the seal's snout as a protective cover. Now the animal can be towed alongside a kayak, weather and ice permitting. The inflated carcass even offers added stability in rough water.

To the eye of a seasoned hunter, Sealing Point's distant mountains serve as a trusted barometer for predicting an ill wind. If these uplands project a shimmering mirage, a warming offshore wind is likely to blow the hunter, his seal, and the ice pack far out to sea. A fast retreat to the beach becomes imperative. But the hunter must first know what mountains to search — *Kasik* looks like a shoulder blade; and *Tigaktolik* has a snow patch resembling an upturned weasel, but only when viewed from out on the ice pack.

The risk and hard work involved in garnering even modest amounts of wild food can

Wearing a traditional qiipaghaq, *Ruby Rookok, an elder of Savoonga, prepares* allpa *(common murre) to feed her family. When ice conditions do not allow hunters to search the sea for marine mammals, birds such as common and thick-billed murres provide alternate sources of meat. (Robert Belous)*

be daunting. Yet the results satisfy a cultural and humanistic need that is elemental to the well-being of Alaska's Native people.

The *Inupiaq* word *nikipiaq* translates simply as "meat." But its real cultural significance to an Inupiat Eskimo reaches well beyond mere table fare, "home cookin'," or even "soul food." *Nikipiaq* speaks of cultural identity through sustenance. Much of modern fare — Twinkies and burgers — cannot supplant the deeper biocultural connection that comes with eating fresh seal meat and warm clams taken from the stomach of a walrus. The natural foods that pass through family hands bring heartwarming renewal with one's own heritage. They help suffuse family history from cold and distant shorelines into living blood and bone. Traditional wild food is nourishment from a harsh earth that is nonetheless a sweet homeland. ●

Island Cycles

It is April on St. Lawrence Island. Winter lies behind, summer beckons ahead. Daylight finally outlasts the night. Off Southwest Cape, spring breezes open leads in the ice. A Siberian Yupik's fancy turns to whales.

"Springtime, during April, is the whaling season," George Noongwook explains. "It's an opportunity to go out and hunt for a bowhead whale. Everyone gets involved, men, women, and children. Whales being pretty big animals, it takes a community effort, pretty much everyone has to get involved."

From Savoonga, the route lies southwest to whaling camp. Weapons and outboard motors have been checked and put in good working order, *umiaks* have been resewn, stores of food prepared and all are hauled to camp.

To move the heavy boats, "some of the boat captains use ivory runners to make it run easier over the ice,"

Food storage in remote areas has always been a challenge. Here, an old meat storage cellar dug from permafrost in Gambell is a reminder of harder times. Before gas-fueled generators provided electricity for freezers, villagers stored meat in these pits kept cold by perpetually frozen soil. Though permafrost aids in food preservation, it can shift house walls by several inches as the ice melts slightly during summer and refreezes in winter. (Chlaus Lotscher)

Culture camps provide a way for Alaska Natives to share the stories and skills their people have developed for living off the land. In August 1999, participants at Camp Qungaayux help Moses Dirks and Michael Lekanoff of Unalaska bring in a Steller sea lion taken off Cape Cheerful. The western stock of Steller sea lions is endangered, but a small subsistence hunt is allowed in the Unalaska area. All parts of the animal were used at the camp including the whiskers for hats and the intestines for jackets. (Scott Darsney)

Noongwook says. But it is backbreaking work all the same.

Once the whaling crews and support teams have assembled at camp, the hunt depends on weather and the whales. Hunters bide time, ranging from camp in pursuit of seals and seabirds, while observers keep a sharp eye out for whales.

"If you're lucky, you might find a whale three to five miles out," Noongwook says. "If there is a lot of open water, you may have to go out 12, 15, 20 miles."

"We do use sails whenever possible. You need a light breeze of 20 knots to get moving when you are pursuing whales."

Umiaks covered in walrus skin are common. "You need a female walrus hide," Noongwook says. "Female hide is thinner and finer, not as many scars as the male hide, so it is naturally good for covering boats. You also need rawhide to tie it to the frame."

Umiaks are especially valued for stalking whales, whose hearing is acute. Skinboats are quiet, withstand damage from ice fairly well, and are easier to repair than aluminum boats.

"Once you strike a whale, after you've killed it, you can use outboard motors to tow your whale in."

Life in whaling camp may be interspersed with leisurely spells. Fog can stymie observers for days. Some years, good hunting weather may be limited to five or ten days during the whole whaling season. But when a whale is sighted, the camp erupts into quiet activity. Crews

dash for boats, which are swiftly manned and launched, and within moments, the hunt is on.

A whaling boat is typically manned by a harpooner in the bow, a helmsman sitting high astern and up to six paddlers seated along the gunwales. When the crew closes on a surfacing whale, the harpooner tries to strike the whale in a vital spot with a toggle-head harpoon, attached to a line with a sealskin float. When the harpoon enters the whale, a triggering mechanism drives a bomb deep inside where it explodes. Several strikes may be needed to kill a whale.

Northwest Alaska residents butcher a walrus on the sea ice off St. Lawrence Island. Both male and female walrus have tusks, which are actually elongated upper canine teeth. (Steve McCutcheon Collection, Anchorage Museum of History and Art)

Bowhead whales may be up to 60 feet long and tip scales at 60 tons. Even with block and tackle, a large whale may have to be flensed, or stripped of blubber and skin, to facilitate hauling it onto the ice for butchering. It may take a full day to butcher a whale and a second day to retrieve meat and *mangtaq* (blubber in Siberian Yupik).

For each crew that joined in the hunt, the take is apportioned into shares and the entire campsite may be covered with the resulting piles of provender.

"Whaling being a community effort, all of that meat and blubber is shared," George Noongwook says, "not only in town but even in outlying areas, in Gambell and other places around the island. And they share what they get, too. They might send a bucket of salmonberries or a bag of dried salmon."

If a crew from Gambell, on the island's northwest tip, should land a bowhead, part of the whale is sure to be shared in Savoonga.

"Last spring, one of the captains succeeded in bringing in a 45-foot whale," Noongwook recalls. "*That* created a lot of excitement."

For St. Lawrence Islanders, hunting whales, walrus, seals, and other

A long history of living off the land enables these Barrow residents to efficiently process a huge bowhead whale. Each village has its own way of butchering a bowhead, with the whaling captain who landed the whale usually getting the choicest portions. The rest is distributed among the residents and sometimes with people of other villages. Some of the meat is also set aside for whaling festivals. (Galen Rowell/Mountain Light)

traditional quarry binds communities and nourishes Siberian Yupik pride and identity. But it does even more: It puts affordable food on the table.

"I'd say about 75 percent of the time when we sit down to eat, we will have some Native food," Noongwook says. "That's mixed with vegetables that we buy from the store, like asparagus, corn, potatoes, or maybe some cheese. That stuff is all flown in and it's pretty expensive. Native food is a lot more gratifying and satisfying, and you develop a taste for it, which makes it hard to replace. It's very healthy food, too."

In cuisine and other respects, life on St. Lawrence Island is a continually evolving blend of old and new. "Lots of folks spend a lot of time bringing in food," Noongwook observes, but families also require cash to support and supplement subsistence activities.

"A majority supplement their income by making ivory arts and crafts, skin sewing, making drums for Eskimo dancing, or with jobs like working for the school district, the City of Savoonga, or the local village IRA [Indian Reorganization Act] Council," Noongwook says. "Right now, there's quite a bit of seasonal construction going on for a water-sewer project. By the end of 2001, everyone will be hooked up to water and sewer. Until now, we've had the old honeybucket system: Haul your own water and haul your own honeybuckets out to the sewage lagoon." While outlying areas will continue the old ways of handling these age-old problems, few Savoongans will miss this particular vanishing custom. "Other seasonal work is in commercial halibut fishing," Noongwook continues.

"There's no port here but there is a packing station where they clean fish, put ice on it and ship it out. The processor comes right up on the beach here in the village."

At present, Noongwook himself oversees the clean-up of abandoned military sites on the island.

"I'm a local liaison between the Native Corporation here in Savoonga and the Alaska District [U.S. Army] Corps of Engineers," he explains. "There are a couple of sites that are being cleaned up right now. One on Northeast Cape was a White Alice [communications] station, a pretty good-sized Air Force site. And there is buried debris near Gambell."

A blue mussel bed is tucked neatly among barnacle-covered rocks along a Kachemak Bay shoreline. Boiled in saltwater over an open fire on a beach, blue mussels add a special spark to an Alaska picnic. (Janet Klein)

Herring Eggs

Haida gather herring eggs (roe) on kelp, which they collect by hand or by using a rake. When they get the eggs to shore, they dry them in the sun, salt them and put them in barrels or freeze them in containers. Small hemlock trees can also be used as a support to trap herring eggs. The saplings are submerged and anchored in bays and along shores where herring are spawning. The trees are left from several hours to a day or two, then retrieved with a grappling hook and hauled into a boat. The branches are covered with herring eggs that can be dried, salted, or frozen. The eggs can also be eaten fresh, coated with butter, hooligan grease, seal oil, or soy sauce.

That's an Army site from the 1950s."

Among the first things St. Lawrence Islanders spend their money on, besides an assortment of store-bought foods, is the gear they need to efficiently hunt, fish, and gather wild food: rifles and ammunition, all-terrain vehicles, outboard motors, gasoline. Some of these things are barged in during summer, when the Bering Sea is ice-free. In summer 2000, gasoline barged to Savoonga costs $2.85 per gallon, compared with about $1.50 in Anchorage. Fuel oil, used to heat homes, costs around $2.25 per gallon.

Some of the handiest new devices in use around the island are GPS or global positioning systems. GPS are hand-held computers that receive satellite signals and convert them into amazingly accurate read-outs of latitude, longitude, and elevation.

"Everyone has gotten hold of one or a couple of GPS systems," Noongwook says. "They are great in fog so you can find your way back to camp. Also, we are required by the Alaska Eskimo Whaling Commission to tell them where you strike a whale, and GPS is a good way to locate where you are at sea."

ABOVE, LEFT: *Katiana Bourdukofsky inspects a wild celery* (Angelica lucida) *stalk on St. Paul Island. The peeled stems of young plants can be eaten raw in seal oil. The leaves can be stored in oil, but the plant's strong flavor can overpower that of milder-tasting foods. (Roy Corral)*

ABOVE: *For centuries the northern fur seals of the Pribilof Islands were the target of commercial and subsistence kills. In 1984, the commercial hunt ceased. Pribilovians still kill about 2,500 annually for subsistence. (Alissa Crandall)*

If outboard motors, exploding-tip harpoons and GPS devices have been absorbed into Native lifeways on St. Lawrence Island, so has English been mixed with the Siberian Yupik tongue.

"Our Native language is shared by people in Savoonga and Gambell and a few places in Chukotka [in the Russian Far East], and it is pretty strong here," Noongwook says. "It's the first language spoken. My grandson is five and he is just starting to speak English now. I think maybe that will change soon because of modern technology like television and the Internet, where you pretty much have to understand and speak English. But with the modern age, I think a lot of kids will become better informed than some of the older folks like myself. And really, that's pretty exciting."

FACING PAGE: *Little Diomeders jig for sculpin during a springtime outing. Sculpin can be simmered in soup or used as bait. (Fred Bruemmer)*

RIGHT: *A line with bait at the end and dangled through a hole in the ice attracts this crab for a lucky fisherman. (Fred Bruemmer)*

Yup'ik Food Words

Fish:
King salmon: *taryaqvak*
Chum salmon: *iqalluk*
Whitefish: *akakiik*
Pike: *'luqruuyak*

Meat:
Caribou: *tuntupiaq*
Moose: *tuntuvak*
Beaver: *paluqtaq*
Brown bear: *taqukaq*

Plants:
Wild rhubarb: *angukaq*
Labrador tea: *ayuq*

— *Adapted from Alaska Native Knowledge Network website*

Asked about problems in Savoonga, Noongwook comes up with only two: "Social disorders like drugs and alcohol. When the Permanent Fund Dividends come out, there is a lot of drinking." He pauses before coming up with a second drawback. "And maybe the weather."

As for what keeps him in Savoonga, Noongwook quickly enumerates three things.

"How people treat you, how people greet you," he says. "A lot of folks are pretty nice and every time you see them they are smiling or waving or giving you a hug. That's what keeps me here, the people are caring. When you are down, they come and comfort you.

"The second reason is the availability of marine resources. You don't have to go very far for good Native foods.

"The third reason has to do with cultural things: storytelling, Native dancing, songs and performances. I like that."

People, subsistence, and culture: Three things in Savoonga that work for George Noongwook.

LEFT: *In a homeland where the nearest vegetable market lies hundreds of miles away, newly emerging green shoots provide welcome variety to a diet of meat and preserved food. Greens can be eaten with seal oil, cooked or fermented. Since fermentation involves no heating, the plants retain their vitamins and minerals, including vitamin C. (Fred Bruemmer)*

FACING PAGE: *A hunter brings home a ringed seal, another of the marine mammals that feed Alaska's coastal residents. At 3 1/2 to 4 1/2 feet and weighing 100 to 200 pounds, ringed seals are the smallest of the state's true seals. (Fred Bruemmer)*

Counting Fish

By Seth Kantner

EDITOR'S NOTE: *Thirty-five-year-old Seth Kantner currently lives with his wife and daughter at Kotzebue. Five years ago he moved here from upriver on the Kobuk where he was raised. He was born in a tiny sod "igloo" with a tunnel entrance. Seth says the dwelling grew to be a sod house with amenities and is now an igloo-style cabin with a plywood floor, sheet metal roof, and glass windows. In winter Seth does odd jobs around Kotzebue, in summer he directs the gardening project for Maniilaq, the non-profit arm of NANA, the Northwest Arctic Native regional corporation. In spring and fall he is at the cabin, continuing to hunt, fish, and gather resources from the land. His brother, Kole, now lives in Seattle. In "Counting Fish" Kantner shows the importance of fish to the rural Alaska pantry. In "Trapping With Dogs" on page 35, Kantner describes what it was like to trap with dogs when he was younger and when the family depended even more on wild resources.*

In the fall, when the dogs still lay in the willows and had not yet been called for their winter's

Frozen and stacked atop a cache that is wiped out each spring by the river's crushing ice during breakup, fish await Kantner's hungry team of huskies. (Seth Kantner)

work, my brother, Kole, and I boated out on the Kobuk River every day, gathering fish for the dogs' winter food. The dogs were ours from the time we were eight or nine. Our parents had gotten rid of their team a few years earlier, but didn't begrudge us the endless catching fish, cutting, stacking, hauling, drying, storing — and worrying about the fish.

Like any bush chore, we checked our net at that comfortable time somewhere between when we felt like it and when it had to be done. It was fun; we got to go in the boat. Our dad didn't allow gas or the motor to be wasted. Boating for pleasure did not happen. The best eddy was about 300 yards from the door. We set a 4-inch-mesh whitefish net at the current line of the eddy, and an old, ratty net hung with 6-inch mesh down a dozen yards to weed out powerful, toothy chum salmon. A spruce pole pounded into the rocks was the shore anchor, a big rock the outer anchor, a Clorox jug the buoy. In the smaller net we caught pike, suckers, grayling, sharpnose and roundnose whitefish, and occasionally arctic charr, sheefish, and *tiktaaliq* (burbot, also known as mudshark). The water was cold and clear, unless it had been raining, then the river was high, muddy, and full of sticks and twisty black roots.

Back on shore, we hauled the

Seth Kantner prepares to check his trap line after a fresh snow. Animal tracks will show him whether fox, lynx, or other furbearers have passed through recently, but the new snow also means he might have to search for buried traps. (Seth Kantner)

washtubs of fish up the bank and cut them, fillets on one side, backbones on the other, and hung them on fish racks to dry for people food and dog food. Heads, guts, and the grayling and three-pound longnosed mud suckers went into the third-of-a-drum dog food cooker where they were cooked immediately. In late August, the noseeums and whitesocks clouded around our eyes and walked up our sleeves as we worked. The fish racks were on the bank near the dogs, which watched us, scratched, or slept. We glanced up occasionally for caribou coming through the yard, or at any whine from the dogs — often the first sign of a bear, moose, porcupine, or other animal approaching. If their noses went up, we dropped our slimy knives, grabbed a willow and whipped the ground — and sometimes the dogs — to keep them silent until we determined the direction, distance, animal, and if hunting was to take place. Meat was food. The season decided if we could keep it, if

we needed it, if the taste was fat and right.

Drying fish was stressful. The dogs got loose at night or slipped their collars, knocked down the racks and ate the fattest trout and whitefish. Mink, ermine, and birds slid fish off the poles. Sometimes a bear borrowed huge armloads. Worst were the days of drizzle or driving rain. If we misjudged an evening and didn't put up the tarps, all was soggy by morning.

At some point in mid-September, Dad would decide it was late enough to start *kuaq*,

burying fish in the grass to ferment. We ate the fish all winter, frozen, fermented, raw, dipped in seal oil. The dogs got theirs too, though not sliced and minus the seal oil. The *kuaq* pile was a welcome relief, just dump the tubs in the grass, organize the fish, make a rough count. One large whitefish equaled one. A grayling and a small pike, one. A large sheefish, three or four. Nothing was exact, or drudgery. It was simply what we did.

We kept our nets out much of the summer. When the water temperature dropped to 33

degrees, we pulled our nets the next day. By then the insides of the boat were iced with fish eggs and slime. Our fingers turned stiff and red and it was nice to have at least one rubber glove. Sometimes a cold night surprised us. In the morning, ice would be frozen out from shore. The boat would be frozen in. Ice pans would wheel down the current, tearing huge holes in the net's meshing.

After the ice froze thick enough to walk a few yards out on, we loaded packs and headed upriver to Paungaqtaugruk. The

LEFT: *Bundled up even on a sunny day in Northwest Alaska, Kole Kantner and Willow Jones hook grayling with homemade fishing poles. (Seth Kantner)*

ABOVE: *Fishing in rural areas isn't limited to summertime. Here, a net is pulled from under river ice and whitefish picked from the web. Physical activity coupled with keeping fingers and toes dry, thus warm, is an on-going challenge when ice fishing. (Seth Kantner)*

water was deep and slow along the sheer bluffs and there whitefish spawned and other fish rested, hunted, and stole each other's eggs.

The walk was two miles and slow, checking the ice with a *tuuq* (ice chisel), scrabbling along cut banks, beating east against willows that leaned west. If snow had fallen, the ice was hard to read, sometimes treacherous.

Along the way big brown bear tracks pressed down the thin snow, as did those of fox, wolf, moose, caribou, mink, and ermine. We carried too much to bring along a rifle and nervously eyed the thickets and the dark draw where Ole Wik's abandoned sod igloo hunkered in the ground.

At Paungaqtaugruk we chopped holes in the ice in a line

parallel with the current. We first stretched a rope under the ice using a long spruce pole with a caribou antler lashed to the end, then drew a net under in the rope's place. The net had small wooden, cork, or plastic floats.

Along the leadline, chunks of antler or old socks filled with rocks kept the net on the bottom. At each end we tied a 20-pound rock to keep the net solidly down and away from the ice. There was five or ten feet of water over the net and it was parallel with the current to avoid slush coming downriver, but it still caught hundreds of milling fish. The first day was long, with a lot of chopping and the air fresh and cold in our lungs. At work's end waited that long trail home.

Ice fishing went on for three weeks or a month. We kept count. We needed 3,000 fish to make it til June and have a few left to dry for camping. Soon the ice froze enough to hitch up the dogs, ride up to the fishing site, and haul fish back on the sled. The fish froze perfectly, like firewood, and were mostly large roundnose whitefish, easy to count, easy to toss two to each dog. After checking the net, my brother and I chipped holes in the ice and hooked grayling to sell to the old ladies 30 miles upriver in Ambler. We wouldn't start our correspondence schoolwork until ice fishing was over.

Each day the catch diminished. The days grew shorter, the ice thicker, the holes harder to keep open. It was time to build a pole cache to store the fish. It was time to start trapping with the dogs. ●

Trapping With Dogs

By Seth Kantner

Morning darkness broke at 10 or 11 a.m. with a glow of orange spreading behind the Waring Mountains. My mom heated leftover caribou meat and oatmeal on the barrel stove. We ate, then shoveled out the caribou-skin door of our sod house. Kole and I raced down the drifts to the dog yard. The wind drifts were deep and ice-hard. Hidden underneath the smooth surface wound the labyrinth of our chipped caves.

The dogs were staked in the willows by the river, below the cornices. They were partially buried and lunged to their feet, shaking off crusted snow, instantly ready and whining to go. The sled and harnesses had drifted over; we shook out the towlines, the canvas sled bag and the apple box of traps, then forced the frozen harnesses into approximate dog shapes. We hitched up brothers Bonehead and Murphy first. During those years, seven or eight dogs were a good-sized team to feed off the country. We had just four dogs. Flint, a hundred-pound malamute and one of the four, only pulled when there was an animal to chase.

This day I started off riding in the sled basket on a caribou skin. That meant Kole had to run behind the sled. The windblown snow was grainy and slow against the runners. We traded positions without stopping. Running was hot, riding chilling. We headed out back, north into the wind, toward the Nuna and Hunt rivers. Our first trap was a 330 Conibear set for river otter in a low, willow cubby at a beaver dam. At the drift covering the dam, without command, the dogs halted and dropped. They rolled and kicked

BELOW: *A strategically placed wire snare awaits an unwary wolf. Trapping has long been the subject of heated debate between groups for and against the practice. (Tom Walker)*

RIGHT: *Sled dogs often jump and bark excitedly at being hooked up to run. To keep the dogs from bolting before he's ready to go, Seth Kantner has wedged an anchor into the snow behind the sled. (Seth Kantner)*

their legs in the air, packing snow under their harnesses. Flint in wheel position closest to the sled was huge and brown and shed at the wrong time of year. He shook off and stretched back toward the sled, eyeing a hunk of caribou and *kuaq* (stink fish) bait in the trapping box. "Flint, lie down." Kole whipped the sled with a

willow. Flint sat, deciding whether snatching a chunk was worth a whipping.

The Conibear, a quick-kill trap, was wired to a buried pole and set with a piece of fish on the trigger wire and a nip of beaver castor nearby on a scent stick. There were no fresh tracks. A gray jay had snapped the trigger but snow kept the jaws from closing. I quickly reset, scooped out the cubby, and we climbed back on the sled. "Get up there. Go ahead." The dogs leapt up. The runners squeaked on the snow and we shouted encouragement.

The next trap site was off the trail, down a narrow path in the

TOP LEFT: *Before the days of snow machines, people used dog teams as transportation, spending time every day to care for their dogs, repair sleds and harnesses, and gather fish and meat for food. Teams are staked in front of a sod dwelling at Cape Thompson where Howard Kantner lived with an elderly Inupiat couple before moving inland to the Kobuk Valley. (Howard Kantner)*

BOTTOM LEFT: *A wolf pelt is auctioned off during Anchorage's annual Fur Rendezvous. Activities like selling furs allow a small cash flow into rural areas that is used to purchase necessities like fuel oil and clothing. (Harry M. Walker)*

creek that flows over three dams into the Nuna. On very cold days when the wind wasn't blowing and sound carried for miles, if a fox or wolverine was in one of the traps — or a moose in the willows — the dogs' ears went up a mile away. The dogs raced down the trail while Kole and I gripped the toprails, expectant yet nervous about moose. Our brake was poor, my .22 rifle prone to a frozen firing pin. The dogs were delirious over a chase. The last time, upriver in Otter Slough, our other wheel dog, Tiger, broke through the front of his harness and got kicked back into the team by a moose. Other times we lost a dog for a day or two while it was chasing caribou.

After the slough at the Nuna, our trail jogged northeast past another beaver lodge. The wind was strong and the dogs kept losing their footing on the polished ice. The sled slid sideways and flipped. We jumped out and turned it back on its runners. Lone stunted spruce beside us were bent and gray and hard to make out in the moving wall of snow. I folded out the wolverine ruff on my hood and pulled the zipper up past the ermine-skin neck warmer I'd sewn in. Kole did the same with his black bear ruff. We broke ice off our eyelashes and shouted the dogs on. The wind got worse. Our faces froze in white patches. The stinging snow melted and froze, crusting our cheeks. We took turns walking in front of Murphy, an arm across our face, pulling on the neckline, leading the dogs down the lakes. They squinted in the wind and were happy to have our company out front.

The last trap site on the trail was protected by willows and a stand of white spruce. Here, at times when I was alone, the team dragged me across the glare ice toward wolverine raging in traps, while I shot the animals with one hand, cursing the many misfires. Now a lynx was caught in a #4 jump trap at the base of a big spruce. I killed it with a blow with the shovel while Kole held the dogs. We stood admiring the cat, melting ice from our face with one bare hand at a time. The dogs rolled and pawed crusted ice off their noses.

The trail home went straight across the tundra and was wind-blown. Snakes of snow whisked around the dogs' legs. Bonehead's testicle swung back and forth, black and frozen in the wind. The sky was getting dark. The orange glow had moved west and from south to north the sky shaded from pastel pink to orange, green, blues, fading finally to black.

At home we unhitched the dogs in blowing snow. Kole shoveled out dogfood. I tossed two rock-hard fish to each dog, grabbed an ax and hurried to

RIGHT: *Trapper Bill Basinski builds a cubby, a trap intended for lynx, with scraps of hide hanging as bait. He wears bunny boots, footwear originally developed for the Army, but now widely used among civilians in Alaska's Bush. (Tom Walker)*

BOTTOM RIGHT: *A trapper sets a leg-hold trap. These traps are attached to a drag, or pole, rather than to a permanent anchor such as a live tree. The furbearer can drag the trap without pulling free; a permanent anchor would create so much resistance that the animal might pull its foot from the trap. (Lon E. Lauber)*

help Kole, who was splitting the dogfood fish down the center. I carried the lynx up to the house. Kole shoveled out the door and we hustled inside before the snow buried the door again.

After dinner we skinned the lynx under the kerosene lamp. While we *uuchun* (fleshed it) and tacked the skin on a stretcher, our dad expertly cut the carcass into meal-sized portions. Lynx was our favorite food, as good as *luck-a-luck* (white-fronted goose). It was a break from caribou. If there was time afterward, we hit our correspondence school books. Kole and I only did school work at night and didn't start until October, after ice fishing was done. We were anxious to

complete the school work for the year before the sun turned back to yellow in February.

When I was 16, rabbits were abundant and furbearers plentiful. Lynx prices were $200 to $600 at the Seattle Fur Exchange, wolverine $350-$450 in the villages, red fox $60-$140, marten as high as $90. We didn't bother the wolves and never set more than 30 traps total, a few miles in each direction. Our expenses were few: a couple dozen traps, wire, chain, ammo, a few nails, and rope. Kole and I sewed our dog collars and harnesses and made our sleds and towlines. More and more each year Kole read books and taught himself math, physics, electronics, while

I ran the dogs and read tracks.

After college, in 1986, I again trapped with dogs. By then the rabbits were gone; fur prices had crashed with the anti-fur campaigns. Times had gone by. Murphy was gone, Bonehead, Flint, Chitina, Achuk, gone. Tiger and Pepper, too. So many dogs, mine and others borrowed, gone. ●

A Measure of Freedom

If many Alaskans harbor romantic dreams of life in the Bush, Joe Delia's 51 years in Skwentna might well inspire a popular novel.

Born in Missouri, Delia was a strapping youth, restless and independent but never afraid of hard labor. He worked his way through school, aided by a football scholarship in college, then set his sites on Yellowknife, Northwest Territories,

LEFT: *Tenacity, spirit, and a love of the outdoors have kept Joe Delia busy in Skwentna for more than 50 years. (Jim Brown)*

ABOVE: *Reports vary on the flavor of gem-studded puffballs, from pleasant to bland to bitter. The taste becomes stronger as the mushrooms mature. (Loren Taft/Alaskan Images)*

on the north shore of Canada's Great Slave Lake.

"About that time, they found gold in Yellowknife," Delia recalls. Following a wartime slump in gold production, Yellowknife in the late 1940s was enjoying a second boom. But Delia didn't strike it rich there.

"I got kicked out of Canada for vagrancy," he says.

Sitka Spruce

Sitka spruce grows throughout much of Southeast and Southcentral Alaska. While not usually thought of as a source of food — although people have chewed spruce pitch as gum — the Haida, Tsimshian, and Alaska Tlingit used to scrape off the slimy cambium and secondary phloem tissue between the wood and the bark, usually in late spring, to eat it fresh or to dry it into cakes for winter. Often they mixed it with berries such as highbush cranberries before drying.

Moving west, Delia decided to try for Alaska. He signed on with the Alaska Steamship Company and began to work his way north at sea. He stopped in Ketchikan for a stint in a salmon processing plant, and ultimately found himself in the Matanuska-Susitna Valley, the area north and east of Anchorage.

"I got a flight in to Big Lake and built a cabin on a nearby lake," he recalls. "I had never seen much snow, and that first winter, all of a sudden, *wham!* We got two feet of snow."

Delia had been struggling to trap with handmade snares and wooden traps, "and I could see that that just wasn't going to cut it," he says. He quickly decided he'd better learn more about trapping and winter survival before he committed himself to life in the boreal woods.

Delia retreated to Anchorage where

he found work with Ward Gay, a bush pilot based at Lake Hood. Soon, Gay introduced him to Max Shellabarger, who was looking for a trapping partner.

"Max was an old-timer from Skwentna, which in those days was real wild country," Delia recalls. "He had come up in the '20s. He'd been around the whole country and he was a real great fellow. He raised cattle and horses, he was a hunting guide, a pilot. He was always taking in kids. And he took me in, along with a couple of Native kids, and he gave us a home."

Thus in 1949, Joe Delia came into the country around Skwentna, some 65 miles northwest of Anchorage, running trap lines under the knowing tutelage of sourdough Max Shellabarger.

Skwentna was then a cluster of cabins that had sprung up near where the Skwentna River flows into the Yentna and thence into the mighty Susitna River. The terrain is lakes, streams, and wooded hills, and in the 1950s it was prime habitat for moose and fur-bearing mammals.

"There had been big fires there sometime around 1945 and the moose population had just exploded when the

Skilled at skinning, Rose Hedlund of Iliamna prepares a porcupine for the kitchen. These large, prickly rodents have no quills on their stomach, easing the task of removing the hide. Summer porcupines are fat; their meat is said to resemble pork. (Roz Goodman)

second growth came in," Delia explains. "The country was rich with moose and wildlife! It had the highest concentration of moose in Alaska at that time."

A willing and quick learner, Delia readily took to life in the Bush. He hunted, trapped, gardened, and fished. He chopped wood and built a cabin. He sold furs for cash and hired out as a big game guide. Along the way, he married and began to raise a family.

Unfortunately, Delia's wife didn't take to life in the great northern woods as he had done. He found himself divorced with two small children to raise. Travel became harder and time away from home was tough to arrange. He gave up big game guiding and, in the mid-1970s, took a job as Skwentna's postmaster.

"I did postal work part of the time and trapped the rest of the day," he recalls.

To tend his trap lines and get around during winter, he raised sled dogs on salmon caught with a fish wheel.

"I ran dogs for a lot of years before they invented snow machines," he says. "And my daughter Christine ran dogs. She is the only girl to ever win the Junior Iditarod."

Delia's devotion to sled dogs did nothing to deflect his interest in snow machines when they hit the market.

"I bought one of the first 12 snow machines in the state," he says. "That would have been in the 1960s. It was called a *Snowtraveler*. I painted out the *S* and *w* and called it a No-traveler. Snow machines are a whole lot better nowadays."

Among Delia's friends from his early days in Alaska was the late Joe Redington Sr., now celebrated as the father of the

John Ivanoff covers fresh moose and bear meat with spruce boughs to keep insects away and to shade the meat. Ivanoff and several male relatives traveled from Akiachak, on the Kuskokwim River near Bethel, to Stony River, many miles upriver, camping and hunting for more than a week. (Chlaus Lotscher)

Extensive wetlands in the Tetlin National Wildlife Refuge support many waterfowl, a source of dietary variety for people living in rural Alaska. Tetlin is road-accessible, and hunting for waterfowl and other game such as moose is common. (George Wuerthner)

Iditarod Trail Sled Dog Race. In 1973, when the first Iditarod race to Nome was staged, Redington tapped Delia to oversee matters in Skwentna.

The Iditarod race from Anchorage to Nome spans more than 1,000 miles, and mushers sign in at more than two dozen checkpoints along the way. At each checkpoint, a checker verifies that the musher has certain mandatory gear, including a sleeping bag, ax and snowshoes, dog booties, cooker and food, and a veterinarian notebook in which race veterinarians record information about the canine athletes.

For the first 25 years of the "Last Great Race on Earth," the checker at Skwentna was Joe Delia. The checkpoint was in his home.

Norma, Joe's second wife, remains a stalwart member of the Skwentna Sweeties, a group of local women who provide free food for mushers as they roar through the otherwise placid village.

Delia met Norma during a fateful visit to Anchorage and the two have been married for 17 years. Mutual friends introduced them.

"I met her sort of by accident," Delia says. "I don't go into town much

but it sort of worked out great."

Norma had come to Anchorage to be near her daughter, who was in the military. At a dinner with friends, Joe was instantly smitten by his new dinner companion.

"I kept on talking to her while I eyeballed her," he says. "Then I invited her out for a fishing trip."

She accepted, came, liked what she saw and decided to stay

By the time Norma settled in Skwentna in 1982, things had begun to change.

"Around 1975, they opened a land program and a few people started to trickle in," Delia recalls. "By the late 1980s, every lake was surrounded by private property and pretty much the mouth of every creek."

The winter population of Skwentna now ranges between 180 and 220, according to postmaster Delia. It varies depending on how good the hunting and

FACING PAGE: A necessary resource for almost all who live close to the land is wood, used for heating homes, cooking, and smoking fish and other meat. This rural resident used a boat to haul spruce logs to his cabin on Judd Lake southwest of Skwentna. (Shelley Schneider)

RIGHT: Putting food up for winter is a crucial part of bush residents' summer activity. Here, smoked red salmon chunks are jarred and will be finished in a pressure cooker for use throughout the year. (Fred Hirschmann)

fishing are and on the need to pursue cash-earning jobs. When fishing is poor or fur prices plummet, more outside work must be found.

Some locals run fishing lodges catering to anglers from Anchorage or from outside the state.

"There's a lot of fishing lodges," Delia says, "every creek seems to have three or four."

The lodges often fill with visitors during the Iditarod race each spring and during the fishing season, gaining some Skwentnans an infusion of cash. Other

locals generate income in different ways.

"There's a couple of big game hunters and guides, some trappers," Delia says. "A lot of people find seasonal jobs in summer to make money. People raise gardens and can vegetables, the guys get their moose and maybe a bear or so. They do okay, but it's not like it was. Years ago, everybody was pretty much living the subsistence lifestyle. Now there's lots of work."

All the growth in Skwentna has reduced Delia's reliance on hunting, fishing, and trapping as well.

"I've moved my trap lines off of lakes because there's so much private property around them now," he says.

Fireweed

Fireweed can be eaten fresh in salads, or boiled when the stalks are tender enough to be broken off with the fingers. Fresh or slightly dried fireweed can be preserved in seal oil. Another way to preserve fireweed is to tie shoots together in bundles and hang them for a few days. They sweeten as they wilt. Then they can be stored in seal oil. In Southeast Alaska, the Haida have traditionally gathered tall stems in spring and eaten them at festivals by splitting each shoot lengthwise with the thumb and sprinkling each piece with sugar. Then they pull pieces several inches long through their teeth, scraping off the tender inner part. The remaining fibrous part is twisted into twine for fish nets.

LEFT: *Louise Woods of Kobuk butchers moose meat with an ulu. This Inupiat village in Northwest Alaska relies on subsistence activities, with whitefish and caribou the other main meat sources for most of the community's 94 people. (Vincent McClelland)*

ABOVE: *Fiddlehead ferns slowly uncurl as they reach for the light of spring. The greens should be gathered when still tightly coiled, while the underground rootstock can be harvested in fall or early spring. Fiddleheads contain thiaminase, a vitamin B-depleting enzyme that is destroyed by cooking. (Alissa Crandall)*

His postal work has grown, too. "Until pretty recently, I lived a subsistence lifestyle," he says. "Anymore, I work eight hours a day at the post office."

If Skwentna's mixed subsistence-cash economy has moved by degrees away from subsistence and toward cash, at least the evolution has brought with it some modern conveniences.

"Most everybody has put in a well," Delia says. "We have running water, indoor toilets, the whole works. A lot of the lodges use heating oil, though most of the locals still heat with wood."

An electric pump, lights, and other appliances require a generator. The lodges and post office have lots of equipment that runs on electric power. "We have three diesel generators," Delia says. "It all takes a lot of maintenance. Seems like you need three of everything to keep things running."

Asked about drawbacks to living in Skwentna, it is problems such as these that spring to Delia's mind.

"Nothing seems to be easy out here," he says. "Something breaks, you run short of parts and you might have to wait a week or more to get them."

A trip to the store, the dentist, or doctor is a major undertaking. Still, the good things outweigh any frustration or inconvenience: the hunting and fishing, the northern lights, and the beauty of Alaska.

"And you're still your own boss, though I have to watch the clock at the post office," Delia says with a laugh.

Chitons

In Southeast Alaska, chitons are harvested year-round whenever big minus tides occur. These marine invertebrates are found near longleaf kelp on flat rock surfaces. The whole top of the animal is black with a light skin film that peels off readily when the chitons are dipped in boiling water. The back has a shell that comes off when it is pried backward. When the shell is removed and the innards (the brown strip) discarded, the rest can be eaten whole. The meat is sweet-tasting and can be dipped in melted butter or other flavoring. It can also be fried in butter, or pickled.

— *Adapted from* Haida Food From Land and Sea *(n.d.)*.

Rocks and bits of shell adhere to the underside of a gumboot chiton, Cryptochiton stelleri, *which has begun to curl into a protective ball. (Janet Klein)*

Transportation hazards abound in Alaska's backcountry. What seemed like a solid snow machine trail on river ice suddenly gave way, pulling Jim Dau's heavy machine down into the air pocket underneath. (Seth Kantner)

"There's a measure of freedom here that's been lost in urban areas.

"It's good country, even if it's not as peaceful and quiet as it was. And some good people have moved here. It's a nice place to live and raise kids."

Alaska's Algae

The term "seaweed" does not do justice to the wealth of edible algae available along many of Alaska's intertidal zones. From "landlady's wig" to "old man's firecrackers" to "neptune's girdle," these algae bring to mind all kinds of images, some that have nothing to do with food. But Alaskans harvest bull kelp and dulse, bladderwrack

and nori, ribbon kelp and sea lettuce, using them dried or fresh, in soups, casseroles, salads, or just munching them plain, as a snack.

For example, dulse, a red algae, is high in protein, vitamins A and B, trace minerals, calcium, magnesium, phosphorus, iron, and potassium. Thoroughly dried and kept in airtight containers, it can be used year-round.

One of Alaska's brown algae species, bladderwrack, also called popweed, creates a flavor like chicken bouillon when its dried or fresh blades are brewed like tea.

Nori, which anyone who has eaten in a Japanese restaurant knows, is the seaweed used in sushi. Alaskans dry it to add a distinctive, salty ocean flavor to egg dishes, dips, or freshly caught fish.

Components of sea vegetables are also used in many modern, processed foods and products. Agar, a gelatinous substance inherent in red algae, thickens processed cheese, mayonnaise, jellies, and puddings. Brown algae, of which Alaska has four species, forms a thickening, stabilizing product that's used in shaving cream, rubber, and paint.

Mekoryuk resident Linda Jean Richards beachcombs for popweed and other edibles in March on Nunivak Island. Popweed, of the species Fucus, *is often used as a soup or sauce thickener; it can also be rapidly sun-dried and stored for later addition to egg dishes or stews. (Daryl Kyra Lee)*

An Aleutian Feast

By Kaarina Stamm

EDITOR'S NOTE: *Kaarina Stamm, who grew up in Finland, came with her family to the tiny Aleut settlement of Nikolski on Umnak Island in 1992. The 32 residents of Nikolski are fortunate to be able to live off the land, especially when fog shrouds their island and no planes can get in. In this photo essay, Kaarina shows readers some of the natural resources that this Aleutian island provides for her family. The children also pick berries and greens: mossberries, salmonberries, wild celery, and clover leaves.*

The Nikolski community net catches a bounty of silver salmon on this September day. (Joni Stamm)

LEFT: *This silver salmon, caught by Joni Stamm, 10 in this photo, is destined for fish pie. I prepare a double pie crust, boil the salmon in salted water until tender, then debone the fish. I cook rice until slightly underdone, chop onions, and layer the salmon, rice, and onions over the bottom crust and season with salt and pepper or fish seasoning. Then I pour three beaten eggs over the layers and add the top crust, which I pierce and brush with an egg. I bake the pie at 425 degrees about 15 minutes, and 350 degrees for another 30 minutes. Other people add hard-boiled eggs, chopped olives, or Veg-all but I prefer the three basic ingredients. (Kaarina Stamm)*

ABOVE: *Timothy Stamm, 14, watched by sister Lydia, 5, washes gumboot chitons for an evening meal. I boil the chitons for fifteen minutes with Tabasco sauce in the water. Other families soak chitons, peel off the back shell and eat them raw. They also eat sea urchins, which they cut open, then dig out the orange eggs with their thumb and eat raw. (Joshua Stamm)*

FACING PAGE: *Our daughter Sara, 17, trapped these red foxes during a night's work at South End Camp, 12 miles from Nikolski. The children get there by walking, riding horseback, or catching a lift with their dad, John, on the Honda. Our family keeps the pelts for decoration; the meat is discarded. (Timothy Stamm)*

RIGHT: *Noah Stamm, 3, shows off trout caught while fishing with sister Sara. Trout are caught by poles off the shore; halibut are usually caught from a skiff although a line on the rocks also works with silver or red salmon as bait. Salmon and trout are caught by rod and reel from shore. (Kaarina Stamm)*

FAR RIGHT: *Occasionally rabbits offer variety for the family diet. Son Timothy, age 13 in this photo, shot this rabbit with a 20-gauge shotgun on Rabbit Island (Anangula Island), about five miles offshore. Rabbit meat is tasty when fried in butter or margarine and seasoned with salt and white pepper. Older rabbits are stewed, and the pelts are discarded. (Sara Stamm)*

First Deer of the Season

By Toby Sullivan

EDITOR'S NOTE: *Toby Sullivan has lived on Kodiak Island for more than 20 years. Every summer, his children and hired crewmembers work at his fish camp in Uganik Bay, 35 miles due west of the town of Kodiak, reaping the benefits of wild fish, greens, berries, and meat.*

The hunting season for Sitka black-tailed deer on Kodiak Island had opened as usual on August 15, but a hard northeast wind came on then too, slinging wind and rain against the island's mountains. For a week the deer kept out of sight, sheltered in the heavy brush on the hillsides, waiting for the rain to stop, for the foggy wind to fade away, for the sun to come back out to dry their fur. My kids, crew, and I waited too, watching the whitecaps in the bay from our commercial salmon fish camp on a beach in Uganik Bay, looking up at the sodden green mountains rising behind the cabin, thinking about the first taste of venison after a summer-long menu of fish and store-bought hamburger. When the weather finally cleared, the change came at night, the overcast swept away in a few hours by a northwest wind coming across Shelikof Strait from mountains on the Katmai coast, and by midnight the stars of autumn shone in a black sky, Orion rising in the south over the trees.

The next day we were out in our 19-foot skiff in the flat light of dawn, checking our gillnet for salmon, and scanning the beach for deer, knowing they would be out in the open after days of rain. We spotted a buck and two does walking down the beach around the point south of our cabin, enjoying the sunshine, oblivious to the low puttering of our outboard motor as we released the net and moved slowly toward them.

Transplanted to Kodiak from Southeast Alaska in the 1920s, Sitka black-tailed have thrived in the lush vegetation and relatively mild winters on Kodiak, and now

Combining a cash income from seasonal commercial fishing with subsistence hunting and plant gathering allows Toby Sullivan to live a rich rural lifestyle at one of his favorite places, Kodiak Island. (Gretchen Nicholson)

Fresh deer meat provides variety each August for Kodiak Island residents. A Sitka black-tailed buck averages 120 pounds, while does weigh in at about 80 pounds. (Harry M. Walker)

number an estimated 50,000 animals. Compared to deer in the contiguous 48 states, they can be amazingly unwary, especially young bucks and does like the ones we were watching. With no predators except man and the occasional brown bear, young deer on Kodiak will frequently stand still and watch intently when approached from seaward, ears cocked forward, curious but unafraid. Older, wiser bucks are usually far more cautious, and must be hunted with stealth on the brushy hillsides, but for personal-use hunting, inexperienced deer on the beaches of Kodiak can be an easy source of food for rural islanders. Kodiak deer are also famous for their mild game flavor and tenderness, compared with deer in other states.

By aiming the boat's bow straight at them, keeping ourselves low in the skiff, and moving at a slow, even rate, we presented a strange but apparently non-threatening silhouette. The slight breeze blew parallel to the beach and carried our scent away from them. The deer stared at us for a few moments, but continued walking slowly down the beach, unsure what we were about but not yet spooked. When we were a hundred yards away my crewman rested his rifle on the bow rail, fired once and dropped the buck. The crash of the rifle shot reverberated against the bluff above the beach but the two does kept their measured pace away from us, alert but still unsure of what was happening. Only as we clambered out of the skiff onto the rocks and began walking up the beach to field-dress the downed buck did they head into alder and high grass above the high tide line and disappear.

That afternoon we called across the bay on the VHF radio, inviting our neighbors for the first deer barbecue of the season, and that night we sat on the beach with them grilling backstrap meat and salmon over a driftwood fire and eating it with roasted potatoes and beach-greens salad. The mountains on the mainland 40 miles away grew dark as a red sun set behind them. As the first stars came out, our children slept in our laps, and we told stories of other fishing seasons in Uganik, other deer hunts on the beaches there, other first-deer-of-the-season barbecues. ●

All This Beauty

It was sled dogs that brought Charlie Campbell into the country around Tanana, following an inner compass that seemed to point the way home.

"I came to Alaska in 1975," he says. "A few years later I was out in Eureka, near Manley [Hot Springs], helping Susan Butcher set up her kennel when she first moved out there. And in the process, I decided I'd like to build a cabin and trap somewhere farther out."

A New Englander by birth, Campbell has long been drawn to northern places "farther out." His family moved to Ontario, Canada, when he was in junior high. He was attending college in Ottawa when his older sister wrote from Fairbanks, asking him to join her in carving a life in Alaska's Interior woods. Campbell responded instantly. He rode the train to Edmonton and hitchhiked the rest of the way to Fairbanks, feeling more at home the farther north he went. He helped his sister build a cabin, then he met Susan Butcher, and in working with the future Iditarod champion, he began to acquire skill in handling dogs.

Life in the country along the Elliott Highway north of Fairbanks was new and exciting, but Campbell's inner compass told him he wasn't yet home. Something drew him on, beyond the road's end in Manley on the Tanana River, deeper into the wooded wildlands along the Yukon River.

"I mushed some dogs out and set up a trap line north of Tanana," he recalls. He built a small cabin and began to trap along the Tozitna River, on the southern flank of the Ray Mountains. He hunted and fished for food, sold his furs for cash, ran his dogs, cut wood, and marveled at the northern lights. Now and then, seeking supplies or a little non-canine companionship, he traveled the 35 miles into town.

LEFT: *At her fish camp on Sixmile Lake, Ruth Koktelash fillets salmon. The fish swim from Bristol Bay up the Kvichak River, through Iliamna Lake, and then up the Newhalen River to reach Sixmile Lake. (Roz Goodman)*

FACING PAGE: *Salmon dry on racks beside the Yukon River near Kaltag, a predominantly Koyukon Athabaskan village of 254 people. Fishing season takes place when the river is ice-free, from mid-May through mid-October. (Alissa Crandall)*

"Tanana was the place where I got my mail, where I went to town," he explains. "And it's the hub of this area. So I sort of gravitated toward Tanana and little by little ended up there. I moved to Tanana in 1980."

The village of Tanana lies in the heart of Alaska's Athabaskan country. It is located two miles downstream from where the Tanana River joins the Yukon.

The country around Tanana includes forested lowlands sprinkled with lakes and wetlands and crossed by streams, rising to the north in rolling ridges of alpine tundra toward the Ray Mountains.

Piled together, these blueberries make an easy snack, and even carry the remains of finger-prints from the person who picked them. The bed of reindeer moss, actually a type of lichen, can be used as survival food. (Greg Syverson)

The confluence of the Yukon and Tanana rivers has long been a prominent place. For centuries, Athabaskans from up and down the two rivers met to trade at *Nuchalawoya*, meaning "between the rivers," a site near the modern-day village of Tanana.

Russian explorers and traders also

stopped near the Tanana's mouth. In the late nineteenth century, Americans built a succession of trading posts in the area, while the Episcopal St. James Mission grew into an important regional school and hospital. Military posts came and went, from Fort Gibbon, built to maintain the Fairbanks-to-Nome telegraph line, to a World War II refueling base for lend-lease planes flying to Russia, to a Cold-War-era

White Alice radio communications site.

The military had left Tanana by 1980, when Charlie Campbell arrived, and two years later the regional hospital, then under the U.S. Public Health Service, closed. Today, Tanana has some 300 residents and local jobs are mostly with the city, the school, or the Native IRA Council. Seasonal work includes commercial fishing on the Yukon River and summer firefighting for the Bureau of Land Management as well as summer construction work, such as building the new washeteria that will provide better self-service laundry and water.

Life has changed over the years for Charlie Campbell, too. He has married, had kids and gotten divorced, and five years ago, he married again. Ruth Althoff, Campbell's wife, also had kids from a previous marriage, and together, the pair is raising six children, ages 7, 9, 9, 11, 11 and 18.

Althoff, a Michigan native, arrived in Tanana in 1988, with her first husband, a teacher. After her marriage broke up, she remained in Tanana with her children.

"I really like it out in the Bush and didn't care to move to Fairbanks," she says simply. "So I just stayed."

Althoff works part-time at the post office and is also a substitute teacher. And of course, the whole family joins in subsistence activities.

"We all go to fish camp together," Althoff says. "I go out trapping by myself. Charlie and I take turns going out [alone] and we take the kids when we can. We went out a little bit with the kids when they were small. We'd pack diapers and the whole works and go out with the sleds," she laughs. "That was quite a thing. Now all but the youngest one can handle a sled, so it's pretty nice."

The couple has two snow machines but they prefer sled dogs for trapping and winter travel.

"We trap pretty much exclusively with dogs because our trap line is in some really rough country, with lots of steep hills and gullies and ditches," Campbell explains. "We do it in November when there isn't much snow on the ground a lot of times, and you'd basically beat up a snow machine. Dogs can handle it better, and they can jump over any little ditch."

Campbell and Althoff have 26 dogs, but relying on sled dogs is becoming less common in Tanana.

"There is this cohort of people doing it and we're aging," Campbell explains. "We're in our forties now and we have kids and village responsibilities, jobs. It's time consuming to keep dogs and it's real hard work. Not that using dogs for transportation is a dying art," he hastens to add. "There are probably 15 or 20 dog teams in Tanana, of which five are really pretty good-sized kennels."

Because the canines eat mainly chum salmon, running trap lines, hauling wood, and winter traveling with dogs makes summer fishing all the more critical.

"We have a fish camp 35 miles up the Yukon," Campbell says. "It's in the Rapids, where the river is narrow and kind of swift and there're lots of good fishing holes. We go there in June and stay most of the time until about the first of September. We fish with a fish wheel for king salmon until the middle or end of July, then there's a short hiatus and then we start fishing chum salmon for the dogs. If there's a commercial opening for kings, we take part in that. We got no commercial season for kings this year and the condition of the fish was not

Skewered with green branches that won't easily burn, fresh caribou ribs and legs sizzle over an open fire near Anaktuvuk Pass in the Brooks Range. (Henry Huntington)

good and the run was not strong. We got to cutting fish for the dogs early, so we were able to meet most of our needs. But I think we are one of maybe two or three families who managed that. It's real serious."

Campbell learned to cut and dry salmon long ago from his Athabaskan neighbors. The fish is filleted, then cut into long, narrow strips, soaked in brine and air-dried on racks before it is smoked for several weeks over a very low fire.

"It's real labor intensive, especially cutting, and it's really kind of an art," Campbell says. In a newspaper column, he once described an Athabaskan woman whose artistry with a blade dazzled him.

"I used to really admire a lady who was one of our fishing neighbors," he wrote. "She could cut fish, talk animatedly, gesture with her knife, smoke a cigarette with a precariously long ash that somehow never got into the fish, and still produce strips about twice as fast as I could."

As fishing winds down, attention in Tanana turns to picking berries and preparing to hunt moose.

"Moose hunting is something that everybody around here does, without

FACING PAGE: Fairbanks resident and trapper Pete Buist inspects a beaver pelt stretched and nailed to a piece of plywood to dry. Beaver are trapped in winter through a hole made in the ice near their house. (Tom Walker)

exception," Campbell observes. "It's real good meat, and with the cost of meat out here, well, without moose you'd probably go without meat. And there aren't very many vegetarians out here, I can tell you."

To support the family's subsistence lifestyle, Campbell does a number of things to rustle up cash. Besides trapping and occasional commercial fishing, he writes a semi-weekly column about life in the Bush for the *Fairbanks Daily News-Miner*. He sometimes works on city planning projects and has done summer firefighting in the past. The newest endeavor for Campbell and Althoff is hosting tourists. They maintain a website to attract visitors interested in guided wilderness backpacking, rafting, or winter dogsled trips into the Ray Mountains.

Like the trips they offer visitors, life is a package deal for Althoff and Campbell, and they're quite happy with the way it

works out. Tanana is a small town, but "we have a good clinic, there's elementary school through high school, a police department, and a fire department," Campbell says.

The village is about one-fifth non-Native, and "relations between Natives and non-Natives are really good. Politics and factionalism are present like anywhere else, but I'm amazed at how cooperatively things get done," Campbell says. "Ruth and I talk about this often: The Athabaskan people we know are about the most tolerant people we've run into anywhere. I'm really at home here."

Asked what he likes best about living in Tanana, Campbell responds, "the way people relate to the country." Then he offers a story.

"There was a funeral here for Maudry Sommer, a well-known person in town. We were walking out toward the graveyard on Mission Hill, at one end

Crab Apple

Malus fusca, or western crab apple, grows in coastal and protected woodlands from the Kenai Peninsula east to Prince William Sound and down through Alaska's Panhandle. They are more commonly used as ornamental trees in the state, but the fruit can be harvested and made into jelly, syrup, or added to pies and other baked goods. Though acidic and tart, they become sweeter and softer the longer they are stored. (Photo by Verna E. Pratt)

A hiker gazes over spruce forest interspersed with muskeg near Lime Village in Southwest Alaska. This type of forest typically supports moose, black bear, and smaller mammals such as squirrels and snowshoe hares, and several species of edible berries. (Chlaus Lotscher)

of town. It was a lovely, warm day, and the graveyard overlooks where the two rivers meet, the Tanana and the Yukon.

We were carrying her coffin over a rather muddy path for maybe a quarter of a mile.

"As we went up the hill, I became aware of this stream of people moving through the woods around us, talking quietly. And I was struck by how at home these people are in the woods, by their low-key approach and their sense of belonging.

"From the grave, you could see out over the river and over many, many miles of unbroken forest. And I thought, 'This is the way it was meant to be, a group of people living in a landscape, and they walk on the Earth as if they belong, as if it were theirs.'"

Campbell pauses for a moment, then breaks his own silence: "So that's what I like about living in Tanana, being a part of that. That, and just being this close to all this beauty."

EDITOR'S NOTE: *Kris Capps is a longtime Alaskan who has written for publications in Alaska and nationwide for the past 20 years. She is a freelance writer and makes her home in Denali Park. In "Fish Camp," she introduces one man's way of life in the Bush.*

Fish Camp

By Kris Capps

Pierre DeMers has two passions in life — the Land and the Lord — and each sustains the other.

Every year, he travels to camps on the Tanana River to fish, pulling in salmon and whitefish to feed his family and his dog team. And every year, that activity allows him to continue his work as a missionary for Wycliffe Bible Translators. By the year 2007, he hopes to have translated the New Testament into Gwich'in, the language of Athabaskans from the Northeast Interior. It is a project he has worked on personally for more than 20 years. To DeMers, the two pursuits are intertwined.

He, his wife, Meggie, and three children lived in the Yukon River village of Venetie for seven years in the early 1980s when he began

Inside the smokehouse, Pierre DeMers continues the steps of processing what will be food for his dog team in the coming year. (Bob Butterfield)

his translation work. He learned how to mush dogs, net fish, and preserve what he caught. He acquired his own dog team in 1981. "It's my recreation," he said. "I sit to the books many, many hours and if I can get out on a dogsled for an hour or so every few days, it clears my head and I can get back to work."

Fishing feeds up to 25 sled dogs. Of the 2,000 fish he generally catches, two-thirds are chum salmon destined for dog food. The rest are coho salmon with a few whitefish. "I try my best to take the best of the fish of any of the species and use them for human consumption," said DeMers.

Fishing also offers a recreational outlet, even though it is physically hard work. When the DeMers family moved to a remote site north of Healy in

1986, they continued their subsistence lifestyle. DeMers, 48, still flies to Venetie once a month for a week of translating and teaching. He slides easily into village life, visiting with friends, helping to build houses and hanging salmon to dry. He says he feels like he is home, for this is where he learned the outdoor skills that now sustain his own family.

When he fishes now, he uses four nets, totaling 600 feet long. Each uses a 150-pound anchor. "You get in shape kind of quick," DeMers laughed. The fishing season itself is short — perhaps two 42-hour periods per week, for two or three weeks. He hauls in thousands of fish during that time. Working as quickly as he can, he hangs 1,000 to 1,500 fish whole, over a smoky fire, to deter flies from laying eggs. He cuts or splits another 500 or 600 salmon before hanging them on a homemade spruce pole rack, covered with a tarp. "You have to set a smoke fire so it lasts all night," he said. "The flies get up earlier than you do in the morning."

There is even an art to making the fire, according to DeMers.

"Smoke with red alder is best," he said. "A little spruce is good, but if you use too much spruce you will get a bitter taste."

He hangs the fish on spruce poles with the meat side facing in toward the pole. "You leave the bark on the poles so that the fish doesn't slip, because one side of the fish is heavier than the other," he said. The meat is then protected from rain and from falling to the ground. Spacing between fish is important. "The more air that can circulate between the fish, the quicker they'll scale up and have a crust of dried fish on the outside. If you can get a crust on it, the flies don't like it. They won't land and lay eggs." Depending on weather, that can take up to a day or longer, he said. He smokes his summer catch two

weeks, his fall catch one week.

"When I fish, everything that I do has been learned from them," he said, of Venetie villagers. "They know how to use the fish in the most efficient way and to preserve it. Preservation is their specialty, because previous to freezers, if you didn't dry it or prepare it in some other way, you lost it. The main enemy, the blowfly, will just take what you

have gotten out of the water, if you don't watch it."

Blowflies are flies that deposit their eggs on meat or in wounds. "We've had years when they are really bad. You can hang up a whole bunch of fish and you come to the fish later on and when you go to use them, they are just hollow shells without any meat in them. The maggots consume the fish."

Connected so closely to the land, DeMers revels in his Alaska lifestyle and doubts he could live that way anywhere else in the country. "It's the people and country combined," he said. "You cannot blame anyone else for your consequences. I think that creates people who understand the basics of life. You are responsible for your own behavior." ●

Transferring his catch from boat to truck bed, DeMers uses a long-handled gaff, taking advantage of upper-body strength and avoiding the back-breaking task of bending down to pick up each fish. (Bob Butterfield)

Hannah Corral eats a just-picked blueberry, a wild fruit that grows in a variety of ecosystems throughout Alaska, from open tundra to shady, mixed forests. (Roy Corral)

Base Camp Kotzebue

About 500 years ago, when Christopher Columbus dropped anchor in the Bahamas, a continent away, on a peninsula jutting into what is now Kotzebue Sound, Inuits from western Alaska and eastern Siberia had been gathering to trade with one another for centuries. The site of *Qikiktagruk*, now the village of Kotzebue, has been a hub of trade among arctic people since time immemorial.

Kotzebue is now home to some 3,000 people. It is still a center of trade and transportation with roots reaching around Kotzebue Sound and up the valleys of the Kobuk, Noatak, and Selawik rivers, deep into the surrounding countryside.

A sizeable community by Alaska standards, Kotzebue is the seat of the state's Northwest Arctic Borough and the heart of NANA, the local Native regional corporation set up by the Alaska Native Claims Settlement Act of 1971. The growing town boasts three schools, including a rural campus of the University of Alaska, a hospital, a fire department, an electrical utility, and municipal services including sewer and water, a regional airport, and some 26

How Does Caribou Meat Compare?

Compared to beef, caribou meat is markedly lower in calories and fat. It is higher in calcium, iron, vitamin C, and cholesterol:

	Caribou	Beef
Energy (calories)	142	232
Total fat (g)	4	15
Calcium (mg)	19	8
Iron (mg)	5	2
Vitamin C (mg)	3	0
Cholesterol (mg)	93	74

(Figures are per 3 oz. of cooked meat.)

— *Source: U.S. Department of Agriculture*

miles of roads. It is also the gateway to Red Dog mine, 90 miles to the northwest in the DeLong Mountains. Red Dog is a world-class lead-zinc-silver mine with monstrous zinc reserves, the largest yet found on Earth.

For all its regional and historical significance, Kotzebue remains today, in vital ways, a village.

"It seems like people want to categorize communities into [having] rural or urban lifestyles," says Alex

Trapping animals such as the arctic fox and selling its luxurious pelt to a fur buyer is one way rural residents combine a bush existence with a cash income. (Chlaus Lotscher)

Whiting, an environmental protection specialist with the Kotzebue (IRA) Council. "Well, the subsistence economy up here is alive and well. Kotzebue may be a city in some aspects, but in other ways, it is the same as every other traditional village in the state."

Whiting, a non-Native, began living in Kotzebue in 1989. His wife, Martha, is an Inupiaq from Kotzebue. The couple met at Sheldon Jackson College, in Sitka. Martha is currently NANA's regional director for economic development and the two have an 8-year-old daughter, Denali.

"I married into a family strongly rooted in the traditional lifestyle," says Whiting, who loves to join his extended

Preserving Sourdock

EDITOR'S NOTE: *Sourdock, or dock, is a favorite natural food wherever it grows in rural Alaska. We thank Anore Jones for permission to excerpt and adapt from her account of processing sourdock in* Nauriat Niginaqtuat *(1983).*

Gather a large bunch of sourdock leaves, sort and clean the leaves. Chop each bunch into 1- to 2-inch pieces. Cut *ugruk* (bearded seal) blubber into 3- to 4-inch strips. Cut 1 pound of blubber for every 15 pounds of greens. Partially rendered, fresh blubber is best, but any kind will work. So will seal oil.

Fill a large pot one quarter full with water and bring to boil. Add blubber. Fill pot with leaves, cover and boil about 10 minutes. Stir wilted leaves and refill pot with more leaves. Continue until pot is full to two inches from rim. Add water as needed to thin mixture so it will not burn. Simmer and stir mixture for about one hour until leaves form puree. You want the sourdock as thick as possible, but not burned. To get [it] this way you must stir it constantly near the end and keep the heat even and low. When thick, it stores and freezes best. During storage it gets thinner.

Cool, then pour into a clean, tight barrel or large, clean plastic container. Stir every day with the masher because this drowns any mold before it can grow and gives the sourdock a smooth, creamy consistency. The masher is made from the trunk and root of a spruce and is used to mash sourdock until it is creamy while still warm.

Be sure to keep the barrel in a cool place and let the mixture ferment until it becomes effervescent, then freeze. Add up to 10 percent boiled blueberries to hasten fermentation and enhance flavor. Add up to 40 percent ripe blackberries and stir in to store for winter.

An edible green, sourdock is characterized by large, sour-tasting leaves that are excellent steamed or in soups. (Verna E. Pratt)

FACING PAGE: *Children in the Bush are raised to help with family activities. Here, Amy Hedlund picks salmon from a net in Iliamna Lake. (Roz Goodman)*

family in subsistence hunting, fishing, and gathering. "My friends are all that way, too. Sure, there are people who work and do the city thing, but there are still a lot of people who live in camps they use throughout the year. Kotzebue itself, for many people, is more or less a base camp."

Kotzebue's population is nearly 80 percent Inupiat. Each summer, many families in the town relocate to camps throughout the region to harvest marine mammals, fish, birds, eggs, plants, and berries. Most people in Kotzebue move back and forth between various camps and the city. But there are a few families who live year-round in the country, pursuing a succession of subsistence opportunities. Shared resources allow some family members to harvest wild food full time while others earn cash to pay for necessary equipment and expenses; the resulting bounty is also shared. More often, however, people like Alex and Martha Whiting find themselves seeking to balance the pull of the country with the demands of jobs.

"The ideal would be to have fewer needs for money so you could spend more time out in the country," Whiting says. "And some people do that, they

March on Nunivak Island is a good time for catching tomcod. Though still winter, the days are getting longer and warmer, and spending hours comfortably on the ice gets easier. (Daryl Kyra Lee)

spend a lot of time out in the country. And even though their domestic resources may be a little thin, they're happier that way."

Jobs in Kotzebue are mostly tied to government and tribal organizations: the city or state; the borough, including the school district; the Native village corporation, Kikiktagruk Inupiat Corporation; NANA; the regional non-profit health corporation, Maniilaq; or the Kotzebue IRA Council, Whiting's employer. Other jobs relate to providing transportation, goods, and services to the dozen or so villages scattered across Northwest Alaska. About 130 Kotzebue residents hold commercial fishing permits, although the local fishery has slumped in recent years with a sharp drop in prices for fish. A number of residents work at Red Dog, commuting between Kotzebue and the mine on a rotating schedule.

Whenever Whiting's job permits, he heads for the countryside to join his family and friends in hunting, fishing, and gathering.

"In the springtime, people go down the coast to hunt *ugruk* [bearded seal] and waterfowl, to catch trout, and to gather bird eggs. Then some move to where it's better salmon fishing, later moving again to where it's better for whitefish. Belugas start showing up in Kotzebue Sound when the ice starts to go out, in June and July.

"In summer, there's opportunistic hunting for caribou: Sometimes they'll come down on the beach to cool off or they'll show up behind camps. And the bulls and fallow cows are fat this time of year. By the end of August, caribou hunting is the prime activity as the herds begin their fall migration. Autumn is also berry-picking season."

Winter brings Whiting's favorite activity, "pursuing the luxurious fur the [arctic] climate produces." It is also a time to "add additional meat to the

---

Traditional Inupiat Calendar

Subsistence calendars around the world follow seasons. This version of a traditional North Slope Inupiat calendar is based on a lunar cycle that dictates when people perform specific tasks, when animals reproduce, and how the sun and moon change the land.

January — moon of the returning sun — *siqinyasaq tatqiq*

February — coldest moon — *izrasugruk tatqiq*

March — moon for bleaching skins — *paniqsiqsiivik tatqiq*

April — moon for beginning whaling — *Agaviksiuvik tatqiq*

May — moon when rivers flow — *suvluravik tatqiq*

June — moon when animals give birth — *irniivik tatqiq*

July — moon when birds raise their young — *inyukuksaivik tatqiq*

August — moon when birds molt — *aqavirvik tatqiq*

September — moon when birds fly south — *tingiivik tatqiq*

October — moon when caribou rut — *nuliavik tatqiq*

November — moon of the setting sun — *nippivik tatqiq*

December — moon with no sun — *siqinrilaq tatqiq*

— Adapted from Alaska Native Knowledge Network

pantry in the form of caribou, moose, and sheep.

"Seal hunting is basically year-round," Whiting continues. "In fall when the spotted seals, ringed seals, and young *ugruk* are catching fish before freeze-up, hunting is done from boats. Some hunting occurs after freeze-up, when seals can be taken from their breathing holes in the thin ice. Later, after the Sound has frozen sufficiently, seals are hunted where open leads form. Then again at breakup time, when they can be found basking on the ice or swimming in between the floes. There's always something going on, always something to hunt."

Whiting's voice becomes passionate as he talks about the rich rural lifestyle that blends subsistence with cash-earning work. In the Bush, he insists, a modest income doesn't necessarily translate into poverty.

"The people who live here and don't go into the country are the impoverished ones," he says. "I don't understand them."

Young Denali Whiting helps with

Annual fish runs from sea to spawning grounds, including this one near Tangle Lakes off the Denali Highway, take place all over Alaska during spring, summer, and fall, filling creeks and rivers with the sound of fins and tails splashing and struggling upstream. (Steve McCutcheon Collection, Anchorage Museum of History and Art)

subsistence activities and enjoys life in the camps with her parents and grand-parents, cousins, uncles, aunts, and friends.

"The time spent at camp is not as much as her mother [spent growing up]," Alex Whiting says, "but there's still that cultural message being passed on, she has that dual thing going on."

Inupiat culture is also being passed through language. Elders are often more comfortable speaking *Inupiaq*, Whiting says, while younger adults tend to speak English with *Inupiaq* words and phrases mixed in. Most children today speak English as their first language, but the tribe has an *Inupiaq* immersion school that is helping to keep the language alive.

Subsistence itself is another powerful force in preserving the *Inupiaq* language.

"The language is the language of the country, the language of hunting," Whiting explains. "There are a lot of things about environmental conditions

— sea ice, for instance — or about animals where there is not a good English translation. And conversely, for city related topics, it's harder to find *Inupiaq* words to use."

In some cases, English words simply are not as concise.

"Hardly anybody says 'bearded seal,'" Whiting notes. "Everybody says *ugruk*."

Whiting has picked up something of the Native cadence in his voice, but he says he is not fluent in *Inupiaq*.

"Sometimes my pronunciation makes them laugh."

He is, however, clearly at home in Kotzebue. Asked about drawbacks to living there, he says, "I can't think of any, except maybe that it is not winter all year." He pauses, then adds with a laugh, "although, I guess I'm about as close to not having summer as you can get."

As for what keeps him in Kotzebue, his answer is swift and simple: "The country."

FACING PAGE: *Taking care not to bruise his catch, David Fox of Judd Lake examines a lingcod. Contrary to what their name implies, lingcod are not true cod, but rather are greenlings. (Shelley Schneider)*

RIGHT: *Caught mainly in commercial fisheries, a few shrimp of various species are hauled up in lightweight pots for personal use. (Steve McCutcheon Collection, Anchorage Museum of History and Art)*

Fresh Alaska Wild Fruit

By Roger Skogen

EDITOR'S NOTE: *Roger Skogen came to Koliganek, on the Nushagak River 65 miles northeast of Dillingham, in 1975. He taught school here for 22 years. Upon retirement in 1997, he and his wife, Vera, opened a lodge for summer guests and a year-round bed and breakfast.*

Walking up the worn path on a sunny mid-July morning to feed my dogs, I notice pineapple weed plants (*Matricaria matricariodes*) forming their distinct yellow-green flowering heads. This is a sure sign that the first berries of this summer's season are finally ready for picking. Fresh fruit is a precious commodity here in Southwest Alaska. Many times we order fresh fruit for shipment by air from Anchorage, but by the time the produce arrives at our doorstep, it is ready for the compost heap. So excitement builds when the first berry crop is ready, and we can pick our own fresh-ripened-on-the-vine Alaska wild fruit.

Salmonberries (*Rubus chamaemorus*), known to some as cloudberries, are the first berries to ripen. A single berry, which resembles an orange raspberry, grows from the top of a short-lobed-leaf tundra plant about six inches tall. Salmonberries are a great source of vitamin C and the seeds provide dietary fiber. In some areas, picking them requires walking long distances on the soft, wet tundra, but this berry is worth the effort and is highly sought by locals. We like to pick our salmonberries when they first ripen and become soft. Then they can be removed from the stem easily, without damaging the plant, thus leaving a healthy plant to bear berries for years to come.

Tasty salmonberries freeze well and are used locally for pie, jam, pudding, and, of course, the local favorite, Yup'ik Eskimo ice cream (*akutaq*). To make salmonberry *akutaq*, first mix 1/2 cup shortening and 1/2 cup sugar in a large bowl. Then add 2 quarts of salmonberries (fresh or thawed) and mix thoroughly. That's it. Other berries, such as blueberries and crowberries can also be mixed in for variety.

One early August afternoon I was watching the first wave of the Mulchatna caribou herd slowly graze its way across the open tundra. As I looked down, I spotted a bush loaded with

Berry-picking sustains Roger and Vera Skogen of Koliganek and provides a source of vitamin C in their diet that they would otherwise have to get through store-bought fruit. (Courtesy Roger Skogen)

beautiful blue berries. Blueberries (Vaccinium) are my favorite. And these were the first of the season. I dropped to my knees and began to graze on these beautiful plump delicacies as I watched the caribou migration, one of nature's most awesome spectacles, pass by.

Blueberries can be found almost everywhere in Alaska, from sunny south slopes of an alpine meadow to a wet tundra bog and most places in between. Stressed out? There is nothing more relaxing than kneeling down in the middle of a loaded blueberry patch and starting to pick. This environment provides a peaceful setting to relax and solve life's problems while each of the five senses is in motion. Freeze this moment in time: the pungent aroma of Labrador tea; a bald eagle riding high on the current of a gentle August breeze; a lone bull caribou making his way on the open tundra going who knows where; the clang of fresh blueberries falling gently into the bucket; and the mouth-watering taste of those berries that never make it to the bucket. There is nothing more peaceful.

The blueberries that happen to make it home are excellent in pies, jams, muffins, cobbler, and akutaq. They can also be used on cereal or just eaten plain with

milk and sugar. My favorite is a fresh blueberry smoothie. Here is how to make one. Mix in a blender 2 cups of fresh blueberries; 2 cups of milk, yogurt, ice cream, or plain water; 1 tablespoon of sugar, honey, or strawberry jam; 1 banana (either fresh, frozen, or overripened). Blend the mixture and drink. Ice or frozen blueberries can be used to make a colder drink.

In late August or early September when the potatoes have been nipped by the first frost, Vera and I load our dog, berry buckets, food, backpacks, and other gear into the boat for a camping trip into the hills to pick blackberries.

The blackberry (Empetrum nigrum), also called mossberry or crowberry, grows on a short, green, mossy plant with narrow, needlelike leaves. Like the blueberry, the blackberry is also found from alpine slopes to wet tundra. In some areas, these plants grow in large patches that resemble a black-green carpet. They are easy to pick and to clean. Blackberries store and freeze well, and are highly valued by locals for akutaq. We enjoy backpacking into the hills to pick them. With fall colors blanketing the hillsides and hunting season in full swing, this is my favorite time of year. I like to pick blackberries for a while, then

glass the valleys and ridges for caribou, moose, or bear while enjoying the beautiful scenery of this Southwest Alaska paradise.

As Vera and I fill our buckets, our dog Reb proudly carries his own backpack with our water and snacks as he smells out the vicinity to make sure it is danger free. When our smaller buckets are filled, they are held about three feet over a larger bucket or plastic bag as the berries are slowly dumped into the wind and cleaned. As the sun moves toward the western sky, we head back to camp with our packs full of berries to store for another winter.

Blackberries are an excellent source of fiber. They also make an outstanding berry cobbler °and I like to use them in a winter smoothie.

Here is my cobbler recipe: Blend together 1/2 cube melted margarine, 1 cup flour, 1/2 cup sugar, 2 teaspoons baking powder, dash of salt, and 1 cup of milk. Mix to the consistency of cake batter. Pour batter into a 7-inch-by-11-inch greased cake pan and sprinkle 1 or more cups of blackberries or blueberries on top. Lightly sprinkle with cinnamon and sugar. Bake at 425 degrees for 30 minutes until a toothpick comes out clean. Cool, top with whipped cream.

The lingonberry (Vaccinium

vitis-idaea), also known as lowbush cranberry, is the last berry of the season to ripen and grows best in open, spruce forest. We like to pick them in mid-September before autumn leaves cover them. Like blackberries, lingonberries grow in bunches and are easy to pick and clean in the wind. They also store well and can be kept in a cool place for a year or more. My favorite use for this berry is in tea.

A cup of lingonberry tea is a good way to prevent a cold. Older berries that have been stored for a while or ones picked late in the season are softer and juicier and work best. To make lingonberry concentrate for tea, simply boil a bunch of berries until they pop, cool the mixture, and squeeze out the juice with cheese cloth or a piece of game bag (a nylon mesh sock also works). Store juice concentrate in a cool place. To make a cup of tea, simply pour a teaspoon of concentrate into a cup and add hot water for a refreshing drink. Lingonberries are also used in pies, jams, cakes, breads, and, of course, akutaq.

As the last autumn leaves fall from the trees and the first winter snow dusts the landscape, our hard work for the season has paid off. We have a variety of fresh Alaska wild fruit to enjoy for another winter. ●

lifestyle gradually evolved into a distinct culture and identity, that of the Nunamiut, literally "people of the land" or "inland people."

In the late nineteenth century, while Yankee whalers prowled the arctic coast, traders and gold-seekers began to invade Northern Alaska. With them came diseases to which Natives had no resistance. Beginning in the late 1880s, epidemics of flu and measles decimated Native populations. Then when northern caribou herds underwent a cyclical decline around the turn of the twentieth century, famine forced Nunamiut families to abandon the Brooks Range. By 1920, nearly all surviving Nunamiut had relocated to coastal areas.

The Great Depression worsened already hard times in Northern Alaska. Natives had grown accustomed to New England whalers and traders and had adopted some of their modern goods and

Change and Perseverance

The Nunamiut or inland Eskimos of the central Brooks Range are unique among Inupiat for their reliance not upon the marine mammals that nourish their coastal cousins but primarily upon herds of caribou.

The story of these people and of Anaktuvuk Pass, their only remaining settlement, is a tale of both cultural change and of profound perseverance.

Sometime in the centuries before U.S. and European contact in Northern Alaska, coastal Inupiat began to move inland to take advantage of the vast herds of caribou that roamed the North Slope. Bands of these people eventually moved into the river valleys and mountain passes of the northern Brooks Range, through which the caribou migrated each spring and fall. In the mountains, they developed a seminomadic lifestyle built around the hunting of caribou. This

tools, including guns and ammunition. The whalers had also provided occasional jobs until around 1915, when the whaling industry in Arctic Alaska collapsed as the number of whales declined and the demand for whale oil and baleen fell. Fur trapping and trading boomed about the time the whalers pulled out, providing Natives with a new source of income and trade goods. But when the Depression hit, the market for furs disappeared, leaving most of the trading posts to close.

While the whaling ships sailed away and the fur traders came and went, caribou herds on the North Slope slowly regained their strength. As the caribou rebuilt their numbers, so did the wolves that preyed upon them. Seeing these developments, Nunamiut scattered along the coast increasingly turned their gaze from the icy sea back toward the land. Between 1935 and 1939, a handful of highly traditional Nunamiut families returned to the mountains. Once again, they trapped wolves, wolverine, and foxes and hunted caribou. Once again, they were Nunamiut, people of the caribou, people of the land.

When the Nunamiut returned to the Brooks Range, at first they resumed their traditional seminomadic life. They hunted caribou year-round but with

Undigested clams from the stomach of a walrus are cleaned, boiled, and eaten by Inupiat people on Little Diomede Island. (Fred Bruemmer)

From spring through fall, Alaska is covered with mushrooms, some edible, some poisonous. Edible varieties can be harvested and combined with other wild foods such as moose, caribou, or snowshoe hare for a tasty soup or stew. Add mushrooms to stir-fries or sauces, or top a salad with the fibrous fungi. Sauté them to add to an omelet.

Some of the more popular mushrooms for picking include Shaggy Mane, Hedgehog, King Bolete, and Puffballs. 'Shroomers must beware, though, for look-alikes that may be deadly if eaten. Even some edible mushrooms, if under-cooked, ingested in conjunction with alcohol, or eaten by someone with a sensitive stomach, can lead to indigestion or worse.

Inky caps grow on the edges of roads and forests, usually in clusters, and dissolve into a mess of black, inky fluid at maturity. Coprinus atramentarius *is edible, but contains a toxin that in conjunction with alcohol causes a temporary, but severe, reaction; this mushroom should not be eaten within one week of consuming alcohol. (Loren Taft/Alaskan Images)*

special focus during migrations. They hunted sheep, fished, took ptarmigan, squirrels, berries, and other food as it became available. They trapped and used furs for clothing and for trade. Each summer, hunting and trading parties visited the coast to hunt seals, walrus, or beluga and to exchange furs for ammunition, flour, sugar, and rice, tobacco, coffee, tea, salt and pepper.

In the late 1940s, pioneer bush pilot Sig Wien convinced a Nunamiut band at Chandler Lake to move to the broad Anaktuvuk River valley. There, Wien could offer them regular air service. He also helped arrange for a temporary school at the site.

At first, the Nunamiut set up their *itchalit* or caribou skin tents on Tulugaq Lake, near the mouth of the Anaktuvuk Valley. They later relocated some 12 miles to the southwest, to the present site of the village of Anaktuvuk Pass.

Anaktuvuk eventually drew virtually all of the Nunamiut in the central Brooks Range. As the community grew, people replaced their *itchalit* with sod houses. In 1951, a post office was established. In 1958, with the help of missionaries, the villagers erected a Presbyterian church.

Two years later, the Bureau of Indian Affairs built a permanent school.

With the new school came mandatory attendance and families were forced to modify their seminomadic ways. Despite their more settled existence, modern tools like the snow machine and all-terrain vehicle soon enabled them to efficiently hunt and gather wild food. If they are no longer nomadic, the Nunamiut remain remarkably mobile. An Anaktuvuk hunter after wolves during the long days of spring may log 200 miles on his snow machine in a single day.

Anaktuvuk Pass today has more than 300 people, and it remains the only Nunamiut settlement. Daily air service delivers mail, household goods, and non-subsistence food and supplies of all kinds.

Anaktuvuk households enjoy satellite cable television and telephones, and the K-12 school has a dedicated Internet connection so students and teachers can exchange email, search the World Wide Web, and maintain their own web site. The village has a fire station with a full-time fire chief, and a health clinic with three health aides, four paramedics, and two ambulances.

In 1986, Simon Paneak Memorial Museum opened to preserve and celebrate Nunamiut history and culture. Archaeologist Grant Spearman is the museum's founding curator. Co-curator Vera Weber assists in documenting Nunamiut history and traditions.

Weber, whose mother is Nunamiut, spent her earliest years in Barrow. She moved to Anaktuvuk Pass when she was 9, in 1973.

"I want people to understand how we live," Weber says, explaining her dedication to the museum. "A lot of people still think we live in igloos and rub noses.

"We are surrounded by mountains," she says. "You can see north and south in the valley. It's a main pathway for caribou herds to migrate. We hunt mostly caribou. We try to get a moose for the family.

"There are rivers and lakes nearby," she continues. "We fish for grayling, arctic charr, and lake trout. We gather berries and edible plants."

Food that is gathered is freely shared among family and friends, and any

Using what food is available, a table is set in Gambell with mangtaq *(whale skin and blubber), carrots, and boiled seal ribs.* (Chlaus Lotscher)

that is left over is available for trade.

"One of the prime tenants of the Inupiat culture is sharing, and it's still strongly held, much observed and practiced," Spearman says. "A person might go hunting and shoot a couple of caribou, and by the time they get home, a lot of it has been given away.

"If it's winter and there isn't enough caribou, we do share what we have," Weber says. "We'll announce on the radio, 'Come and get meat if you want it.' Or hand it out to the family."

Food is also preserved and stored with holiday feasts in mind, Weber says. "Thanksgiving, Christmas, or New Years — there's always a good time to make a feast."

Caribou is preserved both by drying and freezing, and dried caribou is especially prized as a trade good by coastal Inupiat.

"We trade with the coastals for coastal food," Weber says, "for *maktak*, whitefish, walrus or seal and ducks. They favor our dried meat because where we dry it, the air is good. The coastal air is too damp to dry as well and their drying season is too short."

Trading takes place among relatives

Domestic reindeer gather at the edge of a river on the Seward Peninsula, where some Inupiat keep herds as part of a scarce cash economy. Antlers are sold to Asian markets; some of the meat is eaten, but most is processed commercially as sausage. (Chlaus Lotscher)

Laden with vitamin C, lowbush cranberries ripen after the first frost and sometimes remain on the stem well into winter. (Loren Taft/ Alaskan Images)

and friends across the North Slope. Some active trading partnerships have lasted for decades, or even generations.

"It's almost like the whole North Slope is related in some way, close or distant," Weber explains. "And they are friends we grew up with or went to school with, long ago. It's one big, happy family."

The cash economy in Anaktuvuk is limited but, like everywhere else, some income is essential.

"It costs you money to go out and get your free food," Spearman wryly observes. "Snow machines are expensive, and gasoline and replacement parts and all-terrain vehicles."

Income is often shared among extended families to support the family's subsistence activities, just as the food produced is shared in return.

Most good-paying jobs in Anaktuvuk are provided through the North Slope Borough, jobs in administration, public safety, schools. The local Native corporation provides some jobs, and dividends from the corporation and the state infuse more money into the community.

Seasonal construction is sometimes another source of jobs, such as the water and sewer "utilidor" now being built with borough funds. By late 2001, hauling water home in five-gallon jugs

On an early November day in the bite of minus 27 degrees Fahrenheit, an Inupiaq ice-fisherman from the village of Nuiqsut, on the North Slope, opens a hole in the ice of the Colville River. He's checking a net for arctic cisco, which can reach 14 inches. (Fred Hirschmann)

should be a thing of the past, as will hauling buckets of waste.

"I think it will be good that you don't have to haul your bucket out to the road where the sewer truck can pick it up," Weber says. "You'll just press the button and there you go!"

As Anaktuvuk Pass charts a course into the century ahead, improved transportation and communication are reducing the village's isolation. Weber is pursuing college credit through distance learning from two colleges. She is on track to earn a bachelor's degree from the University of Alaska. Weber also travels to Fairbanks for school business and shopping every couple of months.

"It's good to go out and shop at Fred Meyer in Fairbanks but it's always good to come home," she says. "I like the family and friends and the peacefulness of the country compared to the city."

Twenty-two years after Spearman first came to Anaktuvuk as a young archaeologist, he too loves both the people and the place.

"When I came up to the Brooks Range, I just fell in love with it," he recalls. "It was stunning. In wintertime, it was just

starkly beautiful, and the idea that people could live there in winter was a fascinating idea."

Spearman wanted to learn how the Nunamiut had adapted to their remarkable home. And as he studied their history and culture, he fell in love with the people of Anaktuvuk, too.

"This is really a nice group of people," he says. "It's especially fun to see the elders, people the age of your grand-parents, out and active. Here you've got people who are just out there hunting and fishing and cutting up caribou well into their senior years. And that's neat to see, I really appreciate that."

The twentieth century took Alaska Natives throughout the Great Land on a long journey. For the Nunamiut, it began with decimation by disease and famine that drove them as refugees from their mountain homeland. When northern caribou herds recovered, the people deliberately reclaimed their inland home and traditions, eventually settling in the valley of the Anaktuvuk River. Modern tools like snow machines and four-wheelers allowed them to modify their seminomadic ways. Institutions like schools and clinics, and conveniences like heating oil, running water, and sewer lines, airplanes,

Lige Ambrose (left) and Chuck Edwards enjoy a meal cooked over a smoke house fire in Hughes. Strips of moose meat and fish hang above them. (Roy Corral)

Howard Kantner transplants greens after snowmelt in Northwest Alaska. Greens mature quickly under the state's long hours of daylight in summer, and gardeners must keep pace with their harvest. (Seth Kantner)

telephones, and the Internet are all being absorbed. Nunamiut culture is changing, but its beating heart remains: The people of Anaktuvuk are still inland Eskimos, still people of the caribou.

"That's our livelihood," Vera Weber says, "our tradition. We'd like to carry it on into the next generation and the next generation."

Living Off the Land

Some years ago, German film director Werner Herzog spoke at the Anchorage Museum of History and Art. Herzog is best known for his portrayals of obsession, sometimes set deep in the Amazonian rain forest. Now he was visiting Alaska, and a question came from the audience: Why is he drawn to lands of such extremes?

"But Alaska is not extreme," Herzog

Fishermen from Klawock, population 673, on Prince of Wales Island in Southeast, check their subsistence net for salmon. Klawock was traditionally a summer fish camp, and remains an active fishing community today. (Roy Corral)

replied. "This is how the planet was meant to be."

For more than 10,000 years after the great glaciers relaxed their grip on Alaska there was no concept among the people here of living off the land. There was no other way to live.

Ancestral Inupiat and Yupik hunted whales, seals, walrus, birds, and bears, while early Athabaskans hunted moose and caribou and fished bountiful salmon streams. The forebears of Aleuts and Tlingits harvested rich coastal marine resources. In Native communities everywhere, successful hunters and gatherers shared food with relatives and friends and traded with neighboring bands for goods and resources they desired.

Over countless generations, Native knowledge and traditions grew into a rich legacy. Careful observations of wildlife and refined beliefs about the land and its plants and animals were nurtured and passed from generation to generation.

A hallmark of the Native lifestyle was, of necessity, flexibility. When conditions changed and animal populations shifted — when salmon runs were weak or caribou herds crashed or shifted migration routes — the people adapted, moving to new hunting grounds or targeting different quarry. Now and then, technological innovations like the toggle-head harpoon swept across the countryside changing practices yet again.

The most profound shifts came relatively recently, in the wake of contact

with outsiders. Infectious diseases ravaged Native populations. In some places Aleuts and others were enslaved and forced to hunt for foreign masters. Populations of sea otters, whales, and other species crashed when foreign fleets pursued them beyond sustainable limits.

Other results of contact were more benign, or even beneficial: Rifles and exploding harpoons made commercial overhunting possible, but they also made the harvest of subsistence food easier and more efficient.

Henry Huntington has thought about

As part of a Native subsistence fishery for herring roe near Sitka, spruce boughs are secured underwater where eggs from spawning herring can stick to them. The roe-laden boughs are then collected by boat and brought to shore for processing. (Harry M. Walker)

these changes, and about living off the land. He is an arctic researcher and consultant who has lived among some of Alaska's Natives.

"Things have changed, the outward appearance has changed," Huntington

says. "You read letters to the editor and a lot of people are complaining about Natives with their snow machines having subsistence rights. Well to me, that's totally irrelevant. Natives have always been good about using the best tools they have. They're very good at innovating and developing things like the toggle-head harpoon, and so on. If you have a new opportunity, who in their right mind wouldn't use a better harpoon, or a rifle, or a snow machine? But the underlying approach [to living off the land] and the beliefs and so on, I don't think that has changed nearly as much as the outward appearance."

One generational change at work in the Bush is the strengthening of local schools. Unlike their grandparents and even some parents, bush kids today spend a great deal of time in the classroom.

FACING PAGE: *Molly and Seth Perkins help check a net for salmon in Halibut Cove off Kachemak Bay, picking seaweed from the web as they go. Learning that food comes from the land and sea is an important part of growing up in Alaska's rural areas. (Dan Perkins/Cross Fox Photography)*

RIGHT: *Tlingit youth Joshua Hotch, of Klukwan, a village near Haines, shares with his canine friend his delight at having picked so many highbush cranberries. Pungent in autumn air and sour on the tongue, highbush cranberries are used primarily to flavor meats, but can be sweetened for jelly. (Roy Corral)*

Cloudberries, also called salmonberries in some parts of Alaska, are found in western and northern Alaska in muskegs, tundra, and open forests. Some Inupiat mix them with oil and sugar for dessert. (Greg Syverson)

"One respected elder from Inuvik, in Canada, has pointed out that he didn't go to school," Huntington says. "He and his family were out on the land nine or ten months a year. For kids growing up going to school, even taking vacations in the south, a few weeks on the land now and then cannot teach them the lessons it took nine or ten months on the land each year for the elder to accumulate.

"That's not to say that the younger hunters aren't learning things," Huntington goes on. "They have a chance to go out and they are learning. They're just learning in a different way, and of course they are learning different things in school."

It is harder to gage how spiritual connections with the land are being transmitted, but Huntington believes they too are being passed on, if in modified form. Many Natives today are Christian, but traditional values and beliefs honoring animals and the environment have not been supplanted by Christianity so much as blended with it.

"The demonstrative practices that are religious — something like pouring water into a seal's mouth after you have killed it — these may have become a little less obvious," Huntington says. Yet it may be that underlying attitudes about hunting and animals, bedrock beliefs about the nature of life and the spiritual forces that dwell in wild places and in all living things, still reside in the practices and language being handed down.

"There are certainly some younger hunters who are very much in tune with the cultural practices and the traditional beliefs," Huntington says, "and for whom these are extremely important."

Connections with the land are partly unconscious and run deep in anyone who lives in the Bush, non-Native as well as Native. When Joe Delia talks of dealing with problem bears, trapping, or running dogs in Skwentna, he too is sharing a lifetime of experiences that have molded his identity and made him who he is. Rural Alaska leaves an indelible mark on all who love it.

Werner Herzog notwithstanding, Alaska **is** a land of extremes. It is vast and remains overwhelmingly untamed. It encompasses swings of darkness and daylight, depths of cold and clement times, months of icy silence and months

At its maximum size, 21 inches, a kelp greenling, known as a pogie in the Aleutians, adds variety to a family meal. This one was caught at Nikolski, on Umnak Island in the Aleutians. According to Nikolski resident Kaarina Stamm, a pogie is not the tastiest fish but her boys welcome it at fish camp when Sergie Ermeloff fries it in butter and seasons it with salt and garlic pepper. (Sara Stamm)

filled with the tumult of wildlife. From Point Barrow to Ketchikan and even in the urban heart of Anchorage, seasonal changes everywhere in Alaska are hard to ignore.

Alaskans who rely on wild resources are acutely attuned to the seasons; for Native and non-Native alike, their well-being and survival depends upon the world immediately around them. They live closer to the land than the rest of us. It is a closeness we urban Alaskans admire and sometimes pine for.

Life in the Bush does have romance; it is an adventure, but it is also demanding. Still, for those born to it, like George Noongwook and Vera Weber, even the challenges of life are familiar and somehow reassuring. As for those who adopt such a life, like Alex Whiting, Grant Spearman, Charlie Campbell, and Joe Delia, the difficulties are more than offset by the freedom and satisfaction of a life well chosen and well made, and by the beauty of the people and the wild world all around them. ●

Pinkneck Steaks and Steamers on the Half Shell

By Don Cornelius

EDITOR'S NOTE: *Don Cornelius retired from the Alaska Department of Fish and Game in 1994 after a 24-year career as a wildlife and habitat biologist. He currently lives in Petersburg where he shares his love of Alaska's natural history on the explorer-class cruise ship* Sheltered Seas.

A damp coastal fog chills the morning air above Wrangell Narrows south of Petersburg. Here, low tide has unveiled a plain of mud, rock, and sand in front of the home of Liv Ewing and her 11-year-old daughter, Sonja. Clutching buckets and shovels, they slog across the tide flat, eyes scanning for squirting clams or small holes in the substrate. Suddenly a long stream of water erupts from the mud.

"There's one," cries Sonja. Sand flies as she descends on the site with her shovel. Just as fast, she proudly holds up her catch — a tasty steamer (littleneck) clam.

A third generation Petersburg resident, Liv, with her sisters Heidi Lyons and Heather O'Neil, grew up digging clams. "We dug them with our folks and now

Sonja and Liv Ewing anticipate the tasty meal these fresh pinkneck clams will make once the mother-daughter team hauls them home to clean and cook. (Don Cornelius)

we do it with our kids," says Liv. "It's a family tradition."

Like many Southeast Alaska residents, Liv uses clams to spice up her diet. And she knows good food. Liv and Heidi operate a catering service. Twice a week during summer months they serve a complete Norwegian-style dinner for up to 80 tourists from the cruise ship *Sheltered Seas*. Catering for weddings and other special events round out their business. But the catering-service menu does not include clams even though the bivalves hold a special place in Liv's heart.

Her dark eyes glisten as we talk about clams. Pinknecks top her list. "We cut them into a couple of 'steaks,' then bread them with milk, flour, eggs, and crackers."

The look on her face tells the rest of the story. "Of course you have to pound them first, otherwise they're a bit tough, but oh, they taste so ... good."

Steamers hold another soft spot in Liv's heart. These she steams open in boiling water and dips the meat in melted, garlic-flavored butter. She adds a storage tip used by a local seafood market. "Freeze them while they're still alive. It keeps them fresher."

Years ago, Liv's grandparents passed on the secret to getting sand out of fresh clams. Now she just hangs them overboard in seawater in a basket or sack for a couple of days to let them "spit the sand out."

Liv's father, Erling Husvik,

A bucket and shovel are the only tools needed for clam digging, though some people use their hands to dig so they don't accidentally break the shell as the clam heads deeper into the sand. (Don Cornelius)

taught the family to grind up butter clams for chowder or fritters. As for other shellfish, Liv claims she's not excited about cockles or snails because they're tougher and less tasty.

She and Sonja most enjoy digging pinknecks on an outgoing tide. "On a warm day you can see their pink necks right on the surface. Then you have to be quick because they dig really fast."

Liv is mindful of an ever-present danger from eating shellfish. Almost every year, outbreaks of paralytic shellfish poisoning (PSP) cause the Alaska Department of Environmental Conservation (ADEC) to warn about harvesting clams on untested beaches. PSP results from a toxin produced by one of several species of plankton upon which clams and other shellfish feed. Unfortunately, ADEC only tests a few beaches in Kachemak Bay and Cook Inlet in Southcentral Alaska.

Residents of Southeast must either buy tested clams or take their chances. Many, like Liv and

her sisters, do just that. Heidi's husband, Jack Lyons, on the other hand, took a boat-safety class that covered PSP, and now refuses to eat local clams.

Alaska's most famous outbreak of paralytic shellfish poisoning occurred in Poison Cove near Sitka. Here, in 1799, more than 100 Aleut hunters perished after eating blue mussels tainted with the dreaded toxin.

"I go by the 'R rule,'" says Liv. "Only dig clams in months spelled with an 'R' in them."

That rules out clam digging in summer, but Liv says she's never heard of an outbreak of paralytic shellfish poisoning around Petersburg. She figures it's because of the strong currents in Wrangell Narrows.

Still, because of PSP concerns, Liv and her sisters dig most of their clams by the light of a lantern in winter when clam tides occur at night. "Besides," she says, "winter clams are nice and fat, the best eating and safest."

However, ADEC says butter

clams can retain the PSP toxin in their siphons for up to two years, making digging of clams and mussels a risk anytime. The agency says the "R rule" as well as all other folklore precautions are unreliable.

But for now, all thoughts of PSP recede. There's a dimple in the sand ahead and clams squirt all around us. Thoughts of pinkneck steaks and steamers on the half shell are just too much for Liv and Sonja to resist. After all, it's a family tradition. ●

Seal Hunting in Yakutat

By Bertrand J. Adams Sr.

EDITOR'S NOTE: *Bertrand J. Adams Sr., also known as Kadashan, is the author of a short story collection called* This Is Yakutat *and a novel,* When Raven Cries. *He lives in Yakutat.*

When I was nine, I went to fish with my father on the Alsek River, which drains into Dry Bay. I remember on the first day, a couple people had shot several seal near the mouth of the bay where they immediately sank because of the swift current and lack of buoyancy of muddy glacier water. The carcasses drifted over the bar. At low tide they washed ashore on the ocean side and were retrieved. A large bonfire was built. That evening we enjoyed roasted freshly caught king salmon and seal meat. This was a ceremony that had been practiced since time immemorial by the Dry Bay [Tlingit] people.

In the winter seals follow the food supply and they would be seen near the shores in the bays, along the ocean beaches, and in the rivers. In February I noticed that there were more seal in Monti Bay than usual. They had come there to feed on the small smeltlike fish we call candlefish; here the fish spawned on the sandy beaches. In March and April, after the hooligan run was over, the seals had begun to migrate to their breeding areas; they were seen traveling in groups of a dozen or more off Ocean Cape. Hunters had shot them with small-powered rifles;

Harbor seals rest on ice near Hubbard Glacier, north of Yakutat. Alaska Natives have traditionally found many uses for these marine mammals, from eating the meat to burning the oil in lamps to sewing the skins for garments. (Robert E. Johnson)

Bert Adams Sr. is president of the Yakutat Tlingit Tribe. Tlingits are believed to have inhabited Southeast Alaska for about 9,000 years; excavated middens, or ancient refuse piles, reveal evidence of their reliance on marine resources. (Robert E. Johnson)

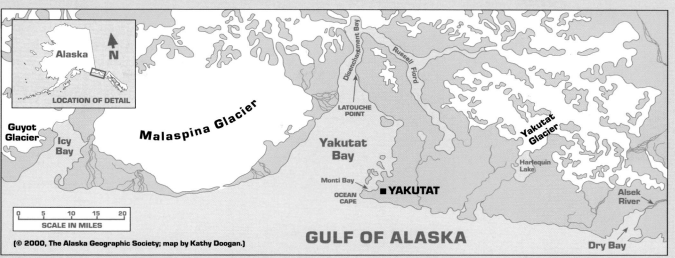

GULF OF ALASKA

(© 2000, The Alaska Geographic Society; map by Kathy Doogan.)

however, I remember stories being told about how, in the earlier days, they would be speared or clubbed. It was difficult to imagine the patience it took to hunt with these weapons because, even now, a seal can get spooky with the threat of a rifle.

When the Natives began to commercial fish, seals became a nuisance to the fishers because they would tear salmon from the nets, leaving huge holes in the web. Because of the plentiful supply of seals in those days the federal government placed a three-dollar bounty on them, but I don't remember people hunting seal just for the bounty. At least in Dry Bay, they were shot mainly for protecting a net or when food or oil was needed.

When I was attending high school in Sitka, the first person I would visit when I came back to Yakutat was my grandmother, Minnie Johnson. She would tell me stories of olden days and feed me the relished Native foods I craved while away. One of my favorites was smoked and dried seal meat that had been preserved in its own oil. Even though I enjoyed the smoked and dried

salmon, which I dipped in seal oil, there was nothing that could compare with seal meat that had been prepared this traditional, special way.

After I graduated from high school in 1957, I wintered in my hometown of Yakutat. In April, I went seal hunting with Joe Nelson in Disenchantment Bay. Joe was a crack shot from a hundred yards away and standing in the boat over choppy waves at that. We shot a dozen seal that day. The bounty from the federal government was for turning in the nose, and the skins were worth ten dollars from a non-Native broker in Yakutat. In 1958, $156, split 60-40, was a good day's wages. We camped that day near Point Latouche, fleshing the seal nearly on top of an old seal camp site where, in the early

days, organized groups of hunters would hunt seal in April or May. Icy Bay and Disenchantment Bay were two major breeding places for seal, and Yakutat residents would spend a week or two in Disenchantment to hunt and prepare their year's supply of smoked meat, render the oil, and flesh the skins, which were used to make prized moccasins and clothing.

After Joe and I had taken care of our seal that day, we built a fire and set up our lean-to tent. We cut slices of seal liver and pieces of fat and strung them onto slim alder branches. We roasted these over the fire and enjoyed a choice meal before retiring into our warm sleeping bags for a good rest that would take us into another day of doing the same. •

Spring Greens

By Carol Biggs

EDITOR'S NOTE: *Carol Biggs consults nature for everything — food, water, healing, photography, writing, educating. Biggs is the author and photographer of introductory pocket trail guides,* Wild Edible and Medicinal Plants: Alaska, Canada, and Pacific Northwest Rainforest, *Volumes 1 and 2. They incorporate her knowledge from more than 25 years of studying wild edible and medicinal plants.*

Shortly after snowmelt in Southeast, which may be from February on depending on winter mildness or harshness, greening sprouts announce the beginning of a new growth cycle, as well as relief for my color-starved winter eyes.

My all time favorite edible and medicinal plant is stinging nettle (*Urtica dioica*), the collection of which has become my ritual celebration of the changing seasons, from winter's colder

RIGHT: *Steamed or dried to eliminate the plant's "sting," nettles are a good source of vitamins A, C, and D. Its fibers were historically woven and twisted together to make string and fishing nets. (Carol Biggs)*

FAR RIGHT: *Carol Biggs owns Alaska Nature Connection. She teaches classes in Juneau and via the Internet on wild edible and medicinal plants and integrated ecology. (Courtesy of Carol Biggs)*

resting cycle to a warmer, friendlier, energetic time. When enough plants are available in one of my favorite collecting sites — an alder-willow-salmonberry avalanche track, or the moist edge of several beach meadows — all I need is a sunny morning and collecting tools, and I'm set for a nature experience that provides satisfaction at many levels. My "tools" consist of a large brown grocery bag inside a plastic grocery bag with handles, scissors, and rubber or garden gloves (for protection from the stingers).

Arriving at my chosen site, I take time to ask the area for permission to harvest some of the plants, and express gratitude

for nature's abundance, freely given. If the nettles have newly emerged, I make sure to leave enough plant so they can continue growing. If they are up several feet, I collect only the top few inches, for the same reason. Sometimes I collect several feet of the plant and hang them to dry and mix with my favorite winter herb tea blend. Though I use only the fresh and dried greens, seeds for tea may be collected in summer and roots in fall for a hair rinse.

My favorite nettle preparation from newly emerged spring shoots is a green-black chlorophyll-loaded blood tonic, with minerals extracted from the moist, rich soil in which nettles grow. Medicinally, nettles help

Tender new leaves of goosetongue can be eaten raw or cooked, though foragers should identify this species with caution as it closely resembles arrow grass, a plant with toxic leaves. (Carol Biggs)

cleanse and nourish kidneys, liver, and the intestinal tract, remove mucous from the lungs, remedy allergies, asthma, and anemia, act as a diuretic, and protect against prostate problems.

To make a blood tonic, I pack a large soup pot full of new spring shoots, pour in enough boiling water to submerge them completely, cool them, then put them in a shady spot outdoors overnight. I refrigerate them for one more night, then squeeze the juice out of the shoots before removing them. After drinking a large glassful of this chlorophyll-rich beverage daily for a week, I freeze whatever liquid remains in a number of containers to drink throughout the year or to add to stews and soups. Chlorophyll repairs tissues, helps neutralize pollution that we eat and breathe, and purifies and strengthens the whole body.

A tonic may also be made in the form of a tea by steeping the shoots for 20 minutes. Because each person's makeup is different, it's wise to start with a small amount of any new herb and check for adverse reactions. I haven't heard of any problems with nettles, if they are prepared properly. Old leaves must not be picked; they develop gritty particles that may irritate the urinary tract.

And I like to steam nettles for an exceptionally nutrient-rich vegetable that tastes similar to spinach. Add fresh king salmon steaks and steamed rice for the gourmet meal of spring. Liquid remaining from both the tonic and steamed nettles makes good soup stock.

Another food-rich habitat, saltwater marshes offer plant diversity favored by geese, other migratory birds, and humans. Goosetongue (*Plantago maritima*), a favorite for any beach and saltwater wetland food forager, may be collected spring through summer, before flowering. This succulent beach vegetable reminds me of salty asparagus, with a texture somewhat like steamed string beans. I prefer eating greens and berries when they naturally mature or ripen because of their maximum nutritional potency. Second best, however, is pulling a package of parboiled goosetongue out of the freezer in December or January when I'm craving vegetables other than those available at the store. Many people jar them, but I like the more natural green from brief parboiling and freezing in airtight plastic bags. I add them to soups, stews, stir-fries, salads, egg dishes, and casseroles.

For anyone living off the land, beach greens (*Honckenya peploides*), also called sea chickweed, and oysterleaf (*Mertensia maritima*) are two sandy or rocky beach edibles well worth harvesting. Versatile beach greens, which are crunchy and taste mild and salty when raw, remain edible through much of the spring and summer. They can be parboiled and frozen as well, and easily included in most dishes. I love their bright greenness in a fresh spring salad. Another beach succulent, oysterleaf, tastes like oysters and may be eaten raw or lightly steamed, and chopped into stir-fries, salads, and omelets. Leaves continue growing until freezeup, offering a tasty snack on cold autumn beach walks.

Southeast Alaska, part of the largest intact temperate rain forest in the world, offers a delightful and nutritious parade of plants available for food and medicine. Taking a lesson from nature's wild creatures, you soon learn how to harvest — selectively. It makes sense to harvest portions of a plant community, never the last one, and only what you need, thereby assuring a continuing supply. •

Bibliography

A Gourmet Guide to Seal Flippers and Salmonberries. Juneau: Juneau Seniors in Action, 1987.

Babcock, Pat, and Diane Shaw. *Cooking in Alaska: The Land of the Midnight Sun*. Norfolk/Virginia Beach: Donning, 1988.

Biggs, Carol R. *Wild, Edible & Medicinal Plants: Alaska, Canada & Pacific Northwest Rainforest*, Vol. 1. Juneau: Carol R. Biggs, 1999.

Breiby, Anecia. *How To Split, Dry and Smoke Salmon*. Anchorage: Circumpolar Press, 1995.

Cogo, Robert, Nora Cogo, and Tupou L. Pulu. *Haida Food From Land and Sea*. Anchorage: Materials Development Center, Rural Education, University of Alaska, n.d.

Foster, Nora R. *Intertidal Bivalves: A Guide to the Common Marine Bivalves of Alaska*. University of Alaska Press, 1991.

Hensel, Chase. *Telling Our Selves: Ethnicity and Discourse in Southwestern Alaska*. New York: Oxford University Press, 1996.

Jones, Anore. *Nauriat Niginaqtuat, Plants That We Eat*. Kotzebue: Anore Jones and Maniilaq Association, 1983.

Kari, Priscilla Russell. *Tanaina Plantlore. Dena'ina K'et'una*. Anchorage: National Park Service, 1987.

O'Clair, Rita M., Sandra C. Lindstrom, and Irwin R. Brodo. *Southeast Alaska's Rocky Shores: Seaweeds and Lichens*. Illustrated by Katherine M. Hocker and Patricia S. Holley. Auke Bay, Alaska: Plant Press, 1996.

Parker, Harriet. *Alaska's Mushrooms: A Practical Guide*. Anchorage: Alaska Northwest Books, 1994.

Pojar, Jim, and Andy MacKinnon, eds. *Plants of the Pacific Northwest Coast: Washington, Oregon, British Columbia and Alaska*. Redmond: Lone Pine Publishing, 1994.

Pratt, Verna E. *Field Guide to Alaskan Wildflowers: A Roadside Guide*. Anchorage: Alaskakrafts, Inc., 1989.

Rennick, Penny, ed. *Native Cultures in Alaska*, Vol. 23, no. 2. Anchorage: Alaska Geographic Society, 1996.

Schofield, Janice J. *Discovering Wild Plants: Alaska, Western Canada, the Northwest*. Illustrated by Richard W. Tyler. Anchorage: Alaska Northwest Books, 1989.

Schroeder, Robert F., David B. Andersen, Rob Bosworth, Judith M. Morris, and John M. Wright. *Subsistence in Alaska: Arctic, Interior, Southcentral, Southwest and Western Regional Summaries*. Technical Paper No. 150. Juneau: Division of Subsistence, Alaska Department of Fish and Game, 1987.

Turner, Nancy J. *Food Plants of Coastal First Peoples*. Royal British Columbia Museum Handbook. Vancouver, B.C., Canada: UBC Press, 1995.

Wolfe, Robert J., Amy W. Paige, and Cheryl L. Scott. *The Subsistence Harvest of Migratory Birds in Alaska*, Technical Paper No. 197. Juneau: Division of Subsistence, Alaska Department of Fish and Game, 1990.

http://arcticcircle.uconn.edu/CulturalViability/Inupiat/changingecon.html (Ethnographic Portraits: Inupiat of Arctic Alaska)

http://fir.state.ak.us/local/akpages/FISH.GAME/ (Alaska Department of Fish and Game)

www.ankn.uaf.edu/akula/Subsistence.html (Alaska Native Knowledge Network)

www.dced.state.ak.us/mra/CF_CIS.html (Department of Community and Economic Development, Community Profiles)

www.epi.hss.state.ak.us/bulletins/ (State of Alaska Epidemiology Bulletins)

Index

STATEMENT OF OWNERSHIP, MANAGEMENT AND CIRCULATION

ALASKA GEOGRAPHIC® is a quarterly publication, home office at P.O. Box 93370, Anchorage, AK 99509. Editor is Penny Rennick. Publisher and owner is The Alaska Geographic Society, a non-profit Alaska organization, P.O. Box 93370, Anchorage AK 99509. *ALASKA GEOGRAPHIC*® has a membership of 4,001.

Total number of copies	10,400
Paid and/or requested circulation	
Sales through dealers, etc.	0
Mail subscription	4,001
Total paid and/or requested circulation	4,001
Free distribution	100
Total distribution	4,116
Copies not distributed (office use, returns, etc.)	6,284
Total	10,400

I certify that the statement above is correct and complete.

—Kathy Doogan, Co-Chair, Alaska Geographic Society

The North Slope, Vol. 1, No. 1. Out of print.
One Man's Wilderness, Vol. 1, No. 2. Out of print.
Admiralty...Island in Contention, Vol. 1, No. 3. $19.95.
Fisheries of the North Pacific, Vol. 1, No. 4. Out of print.
Alaska-Yukon Wild Flowers, Vol. 2, No. 1. Out of print.
Richard Harrington's Yukon, Vol. 2, No. 2. Out of print.
Prince William Sound, Vol. 2, No. 3. Out of print.
Yakutat: The Turbulent Crescent, Vol. 2, No. 4. Out of print.
Glacier Bay: Old Ice, New Land, Vol. 3, No. 1. Out of print.
The Land: Eye of the Storm, Vol. 3, No. 2. Out of print.
Richard Harrington's Antarctic, Vol. 3, No. 3. $19.95.
The Silver Years, Vol. 3, No. 4. $19.95.
Alaska's Volcanoes, Vol. 4, No. 1. Out of print.
The Brooks Range, Vol. 4, No. 2. Out of print.
Kodiak: Island of Change, Vol. 4, No. 3. Out of print.
Wilderness Proposals, Vol. 4, No. 4. Out of print.
Cook Inlet Country, Vol. 5, No. 1. Out of print.
Southeast: Alaska's Panhandle, Vol. 5, No. 2. Out of print.
Bristol Bay Basin, Vol. 5, No. 3. Out of print.
Alaska Whales and Whaling, Vol. 5, No. 4. $19.95.
Yukon-Kuskokwim Delta, Vol. 6, No. 1. Out of print.
Aurora Borealis, Vol. 6, No. 2. $19.95.
Alaska's Native People, Vol. 6, No. 3. $29.95. Limited.
The Stikine River, Vol. 6, No. 4. $9.95.
Alaska's Great Interior, Vol. 7, No. 1. $19.95.
Photographic Geography of Alaska, Vol. 7, No. 2. Out of print.
The Aleutians, Vol. 7, No. 3. Out of print.
Klondike Lost, Vol. 7, No. 4. Out of print.
Wrangell-Saint Elias, Vol. 8, No. 1. $21.95. Limited.
Alaska Mammals, Vol. 8, No. 2. Out of print.
The Kotzebue Basin, Vol. 8, No. 3. Out of print.
Alaska National Interest Lands, Vol. 8, No. 4. $19.95.
* Alaska's Glaciers, Vol. 9, No. 1. Revised 1993. $19.95.
Sitka and Its Ocean/Island World, Vol. 9, No. 2. Out of print.
Islands of the Seals: The Pribilofs, Vol. 9, No. 3. $19.95.
Alaska's Oil/Gas & Minerals Industry, Vol. 9, No. 4. $9.95.
Adventure Roads North, Vol. 10, No. 1. $19.95.
Anchorage and the Cook Inlet Basin, Vol. 10, No. 2. $19.95.
Alaska's Salmon Fisheries, Vol. 10, No. 3. $19.95.
Up the Koyukuk, Vol. 10, No. 4. $9.95.
Nome: City of the Golden Beaches, Vol. 11, No. 1. $19.95.
Alaska's Farms and Gardens, Vol. 11, No. 2. $19.95.
Chilkat River Valley, Vol. 11, No. 3. $9.95.
Alaska Steam, Vol. 11, No. 4. $19.95.
Northwest Territories, Vol. 12, No. 1. $9.95.

Alaska's Forest Resources, Vol. 12, No. 2. $9.95.
Alaska Native Arts and Crafts, Vol. 12, No. 3. $24.95.
Our Arctic Year, Vol. 12, No. 4. $19.95.
* Where Mountains Meet the Sea, Vol. 13, No. 1. $19.95.
Backcountry Alaska, Vol. 13, No. 2. $19.95.
British Columbia's Coast, Vol. 13, No. 3. $9.95.
Lake Clark/Lake Iliamna, Vol. 13, No. 4. Out of print.
Dogs of the North, Vol. 14, No. 1. Out of print.
South/Southeast Alaska, Vol. 14, No. 2. $21.95. Limited.
Alaska's Seward Peninsula, Vol. 14, No. 3. $19.95.
The Upper Yukon Basin, Vol. 14, No. 4. $19.95.
Glacier Bay: Icy Wilderness, Vol. 15, No. 1. $21.95. Limited.
Dawson City, Vol. 15, No. 2. $19.95.
Denali, Vol. 15, No. 3. $19.95.
The Kuskokwim River, Vol. 15, No. 4. $19.95.
Katmai Country, Vol. 16, No. 1. $19.95.
North Slope Now, Vol. 16, No. 2. $9.95.
The Tanana Basin, Vol. 16, No. 3. $19.95.
* The Copper Trail, Vol. 16, No. 4. $19.95.
* The Nushagak Basin, Vol. 17, No. 1. $19.95.
* Juneau, Vol. 17, No. 2. Out of print.
* The Middle Yukon River, Vol. 17, No. 3. $19.95.
* The Lower Yukon River, Vol. 17, No. 4. $19.95.
* Alaska's Weather, Vol. 18, No. 1. $19.95.
* Alaska's Volcanoes, Vol. 18, No. 2. $19.95.
* Admiralty Island: Fortress of Bears, Vol. 18, No. 3. Out of print.
* Unalaska/Dutch Harbor, Vol. 18, No. 4. $19.95. Limited.
* Skagway: A Legacy of Gold, Vol. 19, No. 1. $9.95.
Alaska: The Great Land, Vol. 19, No. 2. $9.95.
Kodiak, Vol. 19, No. 3. Out of print.
Alaska's Railroads, Vol. 19, No. 4. $19.95.
Prince William Sound, Vol. 20, No. 1. $19.95.
Southeast Alaska, Vol. 20, No. 2. $19.95.
Arctic National Wildlife Refuge, Vol. 20, No. 3. $19.95.
Alaska's Bears, Vol. 20, No. 4. $19.95.
The Alaska Peninsula, Vol. 21, No. 1. $19.95.
The Kenai Peninsula, Vol. 21, No. 2. $19.95.
People of Alaska, Vol. 21, No. 3. $19.95.
Prehistoric Alaska, Vol. 21, No. 4. $19.95.
Fairbanks, Vol. 22, No. 1. $19.95.
The Aleutian Islands, Vol. 22, No. 2. $19.95.
Rich Earth: Alaska's Mineral Industry, Vol. 22, No. 3. $19.95.
World War II in Alaska, Vol. 22, No. 4. $19.95.
Anchorage, Vol. 23, No. 1. $21.95.
Native Cultures in Alaska, Vol. 23, No. 2. $19.95.

The Brooks Range, Vol. 23, No. 3. $19.95.
Moose, Caribou and Muskox, Vol. 23, No. 4. $19.95.
Alaska's Southern Panhandle, Vol. 24, No. 1. $19.95.
The Golden Gamble, Vol. 24, No. 2. $19.95.
Commercial Fishing in Alaska, Vol. 24, No. 3. $19.95.
Alaska's Magnificent Eagles, Vol. 24, No. 4. $19.95.
Steve McCutcheon's Alaska, Vol. 25, No. 1. $21.95.
Yukon Territory, Vol. 25, No. 2. $21.95.
Climbing Alaska, Vol. 25, No. 3. $21.95.
Frontier Flight, Vol. 25, No. 4. $21.95.
Restoring Alaska: Legacy of an Oil Spill, Vol. 26, No. 1. $21.95.
World Heritage Wilderness, Vol. 26, No. 2. $21.95.
The Bering Sea, Vol. 26, No. 3. $21.95.
Russian America, Vol. 26, No. 4, $21.95
Best of ALASKA GEOGRAPHIC®, Vol. 27, No. 1, $24.95
Seals, Sea Lions and Sea Otters, Vol. 27, No. 2, $21.95
Painting Alaska, Vol. 27, No. 3, $21.95

* Available in hardback (library binding) — $24.95 each.

PRICES AND AVAILABILITY SUBJECT TO CHANGE

Membership in The Alaska Geographic Society includes a subscription to *ALASKA GEOGRAPHIC®*, the Society's colorful, award-winning quarterly. Contact us for current membership rates or to request a free catalog.

The *ALASKA GEOGRAPHIC®* back issues listed above can be ordered directly from us. **NOTE:** This list was current in late 2000. If more than a year has elapsed since that time, contact us before ordering to check prices and availability of back issues, particularly for books marked "Limited."

When ordering back issues please add $5 for the first book and $2 for each additional book ordered for Priority Mail. Inquire for postage rates to non-U.S. addresses. To order, send your check or money order (U.S. funds) or VISA or MasterCard information (including expiration date and your phone number) with list of titles desired to:

ALASKA GEOGRAPHIC.

P.O. Box 93370 • Anchorage, AK 99509-3370
Phone (907) 562-0164 • Toll free (888) 255-6697
Fax (907) 562-0479 • e-mail: info@akgeo.com

NEXT ISSUE:	VOL. 28, NO. 1

Exploring Alaska's Birds

Alaska is the destination for thousands of migratory birds each spring and summer and is home to several hardy species year-round. This book looks at the habitats, life cycles, migration routes, nesting habits, and behaviors of birds that thrive in the north. Included are sidebars on Alaska's famous birders and the mystery of deformed bills among the state's songbird population. To members spring 2001.

Visit us on the web at
www.akgeo.com